THE COMPLETE GUIDE TO TAROT

THE COMPLETE GUIDE TO TAROT

Master the Cards, Sharpen Your Intuition, and Unlock the Magic Within You

DAWN MARINO

ROCKRIDGE
PRESS

For general information on our other products and services or to obtain technical support, please contact our Customer Care Department within the United States at (866) 744-2665, or outside the United States at (510) 253-0500.

Rockridge Press publishes its books in a variety of electronic and print formats. Some content that appears in print may not be available in electronic books, and vice versa.

TRADEMARKS: Rockridge Press and the Rockridge Press logo are trademarks or registered trademarks of Callisto Media Inc. and/or its affiliates, in the United States and other countries, and may not be used without written permission. All other trademarks are the property of their respective owners. Rockridge Press is not associated with any product or vendor mentioned in this book.

Interior and Cover Designer: Francesca Pacchini
Art Producer: Sara Feinstein
Editor: Mo Mozuch
Production Manager: Holly Haydash

Illustration © 2021 Collaborate Agency.

Paperback ISBN: 978-1-63807-443-4
eBook ISBN: 978-1-63807-226-3
R0

*To my husband, James Lansing, the man responsible
for the ever-growing pile of tarot decks on my shelf.*

CONTENTS

INTRODUCTION viii

PART ONE: THE BUILDING BLOCKS OF TAROT 1

Chapter 1: The Foundations of Tarot   3
Chapter 2: Tarot as a Tool for Personal Growth   13
Chapter 3: Connecting to Your Cards and Preparing Your Deck   23
Chapter 4: Reading the Cards   31
Chapter 5: Sample Tarot Spreads and Readings   45

PART TWO: BRINGING THE CARDS TO LIFE 57

Chapter 6: The Major Arcana   59
Chapter 7: The Minor Arcana: Cups   105
Chapter 8: The Minor Arcana: Pentacles   135
Chapter 9: The Minor Arcana: Swords   165
Chapter 10: The Minor Arcana: Wands   195

A FINAL WORD 225

LIST OF COMMON TAROT SYMBOLS 226

GLOSSARY 230

RESOURCES 231

REFERENCES 233

INDEX 234

INTRODUCTION

Welcome to the beginning of your journey into the art of tarot! Building a relationship with tarot can be a rewarding and empowering experience to carry with you through life. Tarot caught my interest long ago. I was initially drawn to the artwork, the symbolism, and the alluring mystery of the cards. What started out as fascinated dabbling soon turned into serious and extensive study. Today I am a professional tarot reader, offering sessions to help clients gain clarity in their lives so they may move forward for their greatest good. I enjoy offering these messages to others so they can heal and transform their lives.

There are so many beautiful decks out there to express these messages and help us grow and navigate our way. Tarot has given me inspiration, excitement, comfort, and support over the years. There are still moments when I draw a card that manages to take my breath away, whether it's from the amazing artwork, the surprise of the message, or the unexpected synchronicity.

So, how does tarot work? It involves interpreting the message of the cards as it relates to a given question or intention. The tarot deck has 78 cards with images and symbols on each one, and they tell a story. The cards act as a tool for self-growth, healing, decision-making, manifesting, and spiritually connecting to oneself.

Our intuition and inner knowing are crucial components in reading tarot, enabling us to delve deeply into aspects of our lives, selves, and situations. The cards are a foundation, and our intuition and knowledge of the cards help us read the stories and messages presented before us. Tarot is not simply a technique for divination; it enables us to make changes in life so we can follow our dreams, obtain our goals, and find happiness. We are shown likely outcomes and ways to overcome obstacles. Issues of the past, present, or future can be examined, shedding light on information that can help place us on our best path forward. Regular readings help us increase our intuition and recognize patterns or habits in our lives. Tarot helps us know ourselves on a more intimate level.

This book is ideal for tarot beginners, for those seeking to expand their practice, and for advanced readers looking for more complete information and insight into the meanings of the cards. If you are a beginning tarot reader, you will find comprehensive information in this book to help you get started and continue to grow in your practice. You will be introduced to tarot and the history of the practice, as well as basic knowledge of the cards. You will be able to understand the foundations of tarot and the meanings of the cards, along with how to read and interpret the messages for yourself and others. There are sample spreads and readings to use as a guide and reference tool. You will be able to approach tarot with confidence, having formed a detailed understanding of each card.

Please note that while this book is a great tool for working through complicated emotions, feelings, or questions, it is not a substitute for professional medical advice. Any continued or debilitating anxiety, depression, or illness should be addressed by a medical professional. This book is not a replacement for a therapist, medication, or medical treatment.

You are about to start on your journey into the art of tarot! May you discover a whole new side of yourself, inspired by the messages of the cards and the empowerment you gain as you shape your life as you choose. The exciting world of tarot awaits you—you are one card shuffle away from the start of transformation.

THE TOWER

THE HIGH PRIESTESS

3 OF CUPS

ACE OF PENTACLES

PART ONE

THE BUILDING BLOCKS OF TAROT

Tarot is a unique and complex tool that has evolved over the centuries into a sacred practice of self-exploration, discovery, and growth. Mystics turned what was once the card game of tarot into a ritual of divination and inner awareness. The cards can be used to examine life situations, along with our past, present, and potential future. We are given guidance for overcoming obstacles in our best interest. Regular practice builds confidence and empowers a person to make choices from a grounded place for their greatest good. The art of tarot also involves incorporating ritualistic elements that allow a special connection with the cards. There are many ways to make tarot a part of your life, and this section of the book will give you the information you need to help you begin your own personal tarot journey.

CHAPTER 1

THE FOUNDATIONS OF TAROT

TAROT IS USED TO HELP NAVIGATE circumstances and decisions or to explore emotions and concerns that a person may be facing. Today's tarot techniques are rooted in a transformative history cultivated through many contributions over centuries. In this chapter you will learn about tarot, its origins, and the history of how it transformed into what it is today. We'll review the suits, numbers, Arcanas, and court cards to help you know and feel more comfortable with tarot cards. A basic breakdown of the 78 cards in your deck will offer the foundational knowledge of tarot you'll need throughout this book and throughout your exploration of tarot.

WHAT IS TAROT?

Tarot is a tool used to explore specific questions and intentions by reading the interpretations of cards chosen from a tarot deck. Each deck contains 78 cards, broken down into 22 Major Arcana cards and 56 Minor Arcana cards. The Major Arcana represent significant life events, while the Minor Arcana show us details and surrounding elements. Within the Minor Arcana are four suits—Cups, Pentacles, Swords, and Wands—that further illuminate areas of life.

Tarot starts with intentions. Intentions are concepts or specific areas of focus that guide us to examine the goals, dreams, or aspirations we strive to achieve in our life. Intentions are what we hope to accomplish or ways we wish to live. They include subjects or aspects of our lives that we plan to build on and grow. We can work toward manifesting higher alignment—optimal outcomes and states of being—for ourselves through setting intentions. For example, you can set an intention for guidance on how you can be more productive or invite more joy into your life. Areas of focus often include love, career, wealth, health, and personal growth. For more on intentions, see "How to Set Intentions" on page 19.

To use tarot to address intentions, the intentions are formed into questions that are asked, and tarot cards are drawn based on a preselected pattern, called a spread. The cards are then read, or interpreted, to give a message in response to the question asked. For example, perhaps you would like to focus on gratitude, and your intention is to be more appreciative of your blessings. You may ask the cards how you can be more open to expressing gratitude in your life. The card reading may show you ways to find and share appreciation for the beauty in your life. If you are focusing on attracting romance into your life, your intention may be to be more confident in relationships. You may ask the cards how you can become more confident and empowered to attract new love. The cards you draw may reveal suggestions about how to increase your self-worth.

Contrary to common belief, tarot is not rooted in evil or dark magic. Instead, tarot is a tool for communicating or interpreting messages. The cards take on whatever intention you set. You need not be psychic to read tarot; anyone can read the cards. Additionally, messages are never set in stone, so a prediction is not a guaranteed outcome. Energy is always shifting, and we all have free will to change any given situation. Tarot is not a practice to fear but one to embrace and make the most of.

TAROT AS A SPIRITUAL TOOL

Tarot reading can strengthen spirituality by helping readers connect to themselves on a deeper, more conscious level. Reading tarot enables a person to gain a more empowered sense of self through emotional exploration. This practice offers opportunities to understand the energy behind scenarios and how to shift one's perspective to a more empathetic and spiritually aware viewpoint. The cards act as a helpful spiritual tool to align a person to their path for their greatest, highest good.

Tarot can be a ritual that holds a spiritual essence, providing structured guidance into deeper inner awareness. Regular tarot reading develops mindfulness as well as strengthened and increased intuition. Tarot card readings have calming and meditative elements, such as setting up a sacred space for practicing, focusing on a subject while shuffling, and using inner guidance in the tarot interpretations. Regular practice increases a person's spiritual and intuitive connection to oneself when exploring emotions, feelings, reactions, and instincts.

Tarot also intertwines with other spiritual practices, enhancing both these practices and the tarot readings. Spiritual practices that connect to tarot include kabbalah, crystals, numerology, astrology, chakras, witchcraft, and more. To learn about other spiritual practices connected to tarot, please see "Tarot and Other Spiritual and Healing Traditions" on page 17.

THE ORIGINS OF TAROT

Tarot decks were not originally designed for mystical exploration; they were used in a card game. People started using tarot for fortune-telling and divination in the 1700s in France. The cards became linked with the mysteries of the occult, and the tarot symbols were connected to Egyptian mythology as tools of divination. Specific meanings were assigned to the cards, and methods of placing the cards in spreads for divination developed.

Occultists started attributing more meaning to each card for divination purposes and publishing various writings on the symbolic references of the tarot cards. By the early 1900s some people started teaching their own interpretations of tarot. Using the cards for mystical, divinatory, and fortune-telling activities grew in popularity.

Over time the cards also evolved as a psychological tool for self and spiritual awareness, guidance, and personal development. After 1970 the strict meanings for each card were loosened, and tarot reading embraced a relaxed, more fluid way of interpreting the messages of the cards. This allowed tarot to become more accessible and interactive, creating an opportunity to shape the practice to fit one's needs. Today, tarot offers paths to self-discovery, healing, spiritual growth, and personal development, along with the mystical and occult elements from centuries past. Tarot enables a person to connect to themselves on a deeper level spiritually, mentally, and emotionally. Inner growth and personal development are achieved through the guidance of the cards.

THE HISTORY OF THE TAROT DECK

The tarot deck originated in Italy around the 14th century as a card game known as *tarocchi appropriati*, which was a variation of *mamluk*, a Turkish card game. Turkish mamluk cards were designed as playing cards with the suits of Cups, Swords, Coins, and Sticks. In Italy, the card designs were inspired by costumed characters in the local carnival parade. Later, wealthy Italian families commissioned artists to design the cards, incorporating more cards into the deck through the years. Over time, the card game expanded across Europe; when it reached France, the name changed from *tarocchi* to *tarot*.

The decks slowly grew into today's 78-card deck. The artwork on the cards did not evolve and take on esoteric meanings until centuries later. The deck progressed to having Major and Minor Arcana, plus the four suits of Cups, Pentacles, Swords, and Wands. That formula remains the foundation for the cards today.

The Rider-Waite-Smith Deck

The Rider-Waite-Smith deck is considered the most popular tarot deck. It was created by the mystic A. E. Waite in 1909 with artwork he commissioned from a clairvoyant named Pamela Colman Smith. (The deck was originally published by the Rider Company—hence the name.) The images on the cards were drawn by Smith in a way that conveyed the meanings Waite attributed to the deck.

Waite's interpretation of the deck is inspired by Egyptian mythology, Christian symbolism, the Hermetic Order of the Golden Dawn (a secret society devoted to the occult, metaphysics, and paranormal activities), and the French occultist Ettellia's writings on the spiritual meanings of the cards. The Rider-Waite-Smith deck is well known, and the card meanings serve as a foundation for learning tarot. The deck has inspired many other tarot decks, and its art and symbolism are a significant part of learning about and practicing tarot.

Tarot Decks Have Evolved over Time

Tarot decks have evolved to be more inclusive and diverse in their characters and the artwork that portrays the archetypes (the different characteristics of people or aspects of our lives in tarot readings). Many decks have their foundation in the Rider-Waite-Smith deck but use more contemporary depictions. There are also some decks that deviate from tradition with very different interpretations and images. We'll discuss how to feel empowered and confident about your deck selection in chapter 3.

AN OVERVIEW OF THE 78 CARDS

The 78 cards that make up a tarot deck are divided into in 22 Major Arcana (major mysteries) and 56 Minor Arcana (minor mysteries). The Major Arcana represent different archetypes of personalities, behaviors, patterns, and tendencies. The Minor Arcana cards are divided into four suits. Each suit contains 10 numbered cards and four court cards: the Page, Knight, Queen, and King.

Each tarot card has an artistic image that is full of symbols that often repeat in many of the cards. The symbolism helps provide a more detailed understanding of situations during readings. Mountains, bodies of water, salamanders, infinity symbols, and crowns are all examples of symbols on tarot cards. Color themes within the art can also be symbolic. Numerology enhances readings, as the numbers on the cards hold significant meanings. The card numbers also show what stage a person or situation may be at in their journey. For example, nine suggests a situation is nearing completion but is not quite done yet.

The 22 Major Arcana Cards

The 22 Major Arcana cards follow the journey of The Fool. The Fool starts out with simplicity and innocence, a new beginning, and completes the journey with The World. In every deck, the Major

Arcana follow The Fool's Journey from start to finish, and the 22 cards in that journey tell a story for the reader to interpret.

The archetypes of the Major Arcana cards symbolize significant life events, personality traits, patterns, and behaviors, showing the spiritual evolution and life lessons we encounter along the way. These themes are typical occurrences in our lives, and the cards show us how to navigate them and align ourselves for our greatest good. Through the cards we can see where we have been, where we currently are, where we may be headed, and how to shift our circumstances for the best likely outcome.

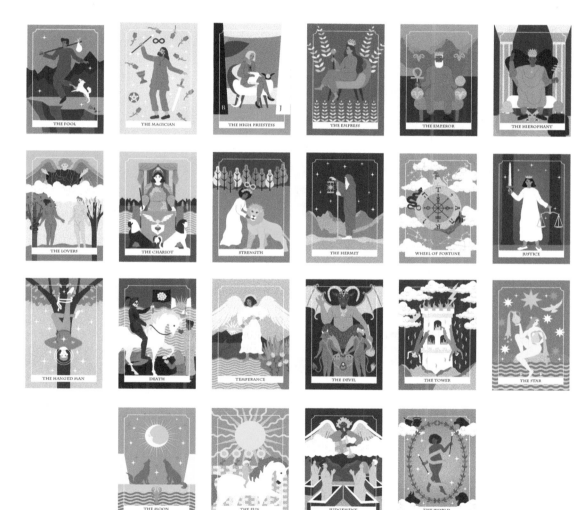

The 56 Minor Arcana Cards

There are 56 Minor Arcana cards, divided into four suits—Cups, Pentacles, Swords and Wands—that represent different emotions, feelings, habits, thoughts, and other elements we may embody at a given time. The Minor cards interact with the Major cards by showing temporary influences in our lives that reflect our day-to-day experiences. We are able to gain insight into elements such as our careers, material possessions, health, wealth, relationships, ideas, emotions, and spirituality through the Minor cards. Tarot readings show what may be affecting these things, why, and ways to work through them. The interactions of the Minor cards relate to the influences of the Major cards, shedding light on thoughts, actions, and feelings associated with an experience or situation so we can understand the best course of action.

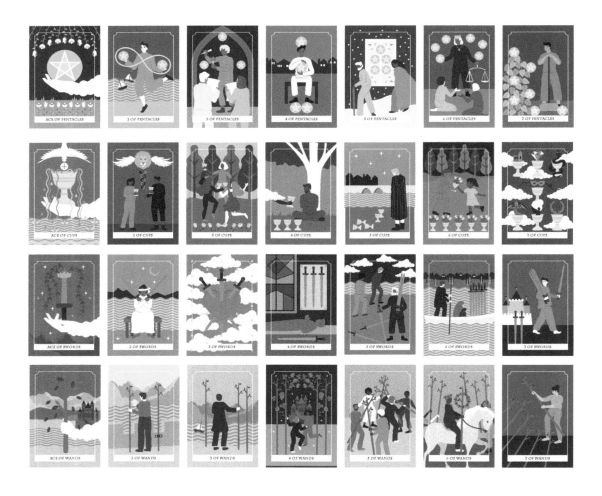

THE NUMBERS (ACE TO TEN)

The numbers on tarot cards have significant numerological meanings that date back to ancient times. These meanings offer greater detail when reading tarot and can show how far along a person is in their journey. Ace (or one) means new beginnings, two represents balance, three shows creativity, four indicates a foundation, five signifies change, six represents harmony, seven reveals contemplation, eight means mastery, nine represents accomplishment, and ten indicates the end or completion.

THE COURT CARDS (PAGE, KNIGHT, QUEEN, KING)

The 16 court cards often represent people in a particular situation or different characteristics and personality traits we embody. Pages represent youth, messages, or communication and new opportunities. Knights signify action, energy, and movement. Queens often relate to nurturing, creativity, and power. Kings are associated with control, leadership, and responsibility.

THE SUITS

There are 14 cards in each suit (ace to king), and the suit and rank are combined for a fuller meaning in a reading.

→ **Cups** signify the depth of our emotions and intuition. Cups represent relationships, as well, and the emotional aspects connected to them. Creativity is also an important element of the Cup cards.

→ **Pentacles** are talismans—sometimes shown as discs inscribed with a pentagram. These cards represent our earthly and material possessions, along with attributes such as career, finances, and home. Pentacles also are associated with our health, our families, and the manifestation of our goals.

→ **Swords** stand for intellect, challenges, and mental aspects. Swords often show us conflict, change, or power. In readings, Swords can point to decisions to be made or a need for clarity.

→ **Wands** depict inspiration, action, and energy. This suit is full of ideas and empowerment. Wands often indicate ambition, passion, and fiery enthusiasm. There is also an impulsive element, as well as a spiritual one, to the Wands.

LET THE TAROT BE YOUR TEACHER

Tarot can teach you lessons and give insight into your life. Every reading offers a new and unique opportunity to connect more deeply to yourself. When you are facing challenges, tarot can offer guidance and provide direction. As you work with the cards, you will start to feel more comfortable. Allow the deck to guide you and the cards to tell you a story.

The images, the symbols, the colors, and the numbers will enable you to tap into your intuition and your inner knowing. Examine the cards and the sequence in which you have drawn them. Let tarot show you the way as you interpret the message presented to you. The more you practice reading, the more you will experience personal growth and learn about yourself.

TIPS FOR BEGINNERS

◆ Focus on your intentions and ask a clear, open-ended question.
◆ Choose a spread to help bring clarity and detail to your reading.
◆ Practice regularly and journal key words to help you understand the cards.
◆ Allow the reading to flow naturally; relax and keep it simple.
◆ Shuffle your cards thoroughly and clear your deck regularly.
◆ Trust your intuition! Do not doubt yourself as you interpret the messages.

You Will Learn Something New Every Time

One of the most exciting elements of practicing tarot is how you can learn something new every time you do a reading! The energy of a situation is always changing, and the cards you pull may offer subtle differences each time you read them. The imagery and artwork on the cards is full of symbolism to explore, and you may find connections and patterns between the cards that you never noticed before. The placement of the cards in a spread can also affect the meaning of the message.

Perhaps a reading does not make sense to you until much later, after a situation is resolved, when suddenly the cards you pulled resonate and you understand their meaning. You may find that certain cards show up almost daily for a period of time until an issue is addressed or that cards jump out to be noticed as you shuffle. Tarot offers the opportunity to surprise yourself with what you may learn about yourself, your life, and the events that shape you.

HOW TO USE THIS BOOK

This book provides information to help you understand tarot so that you can practice comfortably and with confidence. In the chapters ahead you will learn how to prepare your deck, your space, and yourself for readings. You will find the meanings and descriptions of each card for your reference, as well as information on how to read the cards. There are sample spreads to guide you so that you can set up structured readings.

You will learn the different uses and aspects of tarot reading, along with spiritual and healing modalities you can incorporate into your practice. How to set your intentions before a tarot reading is explained, too, so that you are prepared to start working with your cards. Allow this book to be an instructional guide to your tarot practice, as well as a point of reference so you can grow as a reader.

Each card is examined, with key words for reference and a discussion of the meanings both when you pull the card upright and when it is reversed. You will also find the numerological, astrological, and symbolic attributes of each card, as well as their colors and elements. This book breaks down each card's meaning for love and relationships, career and wealth, success and happiness, and other possible areas.

LET'S GET STARTED

Tarot has a history that laid the foundation for what the practice has become today. What began as a card game to pass the time has turned into a tool for divination, self-discovery, and personal growth. The contributions of well-known mystics helped develop a method of card reading to explore aspects of a person's life through the Major and Minor Arcanas. The four suits offer the finer details of a situation, with the court cards examining personality traits and characteristics.

Tarot has been transformed into a deeply personal tool or guide to navigate through the challenges in life and offer support for manifesting your goals. Now that you are familiar with the origins of tarot, it's time to get started!

CHAPTER 2

TAROT AS A TOOL FOR PERSONAL GROWTH

PRACTICING TAROT CAN HAVE A POSITIVE impact on your life. Reading the cards for yourself offers the opportunity for personal growth, spiritual connections, and increased intuition. Contemplating your past, your present, and where you are currently headed gives insight into your thoughts, behaviors, and patterns. The cards suggest solutions and ways to overcome obstacles so that you can become more empowered and grounded.

This chapter will explain the different ways tarot enhances your personal development and deepens your connection to yourself. You will also learn how to incorporate the cards into other spiritual and healing traditions. You will come to understand the crucial step of setting your intentions before a reading, along with the ways tarot can help align you with your most ideal path in life.

HOW TAROT CAN AFFECT YOUR LIFE

Tarot can offer comfort and support or strength when you need reassurance. Regular tarot practice allows you to create your own ritual to look forward to. Your spiritual connection deepens, your intuition expands, and you become more confident and empowered when it comes to trusting your instincts. Tarot shapes your emotional responses, helping you shift your perspective and become more emotionally aware. Journaling about your readings is an expressive activity that offers a creative outlet and provokes deeper thinking.

Your inner knowing and wisdom are enhanced by regularly connecting with yourself through the cards. As you lay out cards to help view situations and choose which path feels best aligned with your needs, you will notice that you're becoming more discerning. Self-exploration enables you to get more in touch with yourself and understand yourself and others on a deeper level. There is a reflective, meditative element to tarot in which you can sit with a card to ponder how the meaning applies to you. The impact of tarot on your life can be very empowering, exciting—and also fun!

Tarot Provides Space for Reflection, Intuition, and Grounding

Reading tarot provides a way to reflect on yourself and situations. You can draw one card daily to reflect on, or you can journal about the messages of your readings. This enables you to contemplate and consider the entirety of yourself and your circumstances. Regular practice strengthens and expands your intuition and helps you trust your instincts. The empowerment you gain from reading tarot can be very grounding, keeping you present and focused.

Tarot Encourages You to Acknowledge Your Past, Present, and Future

Readings that cover the past, present, and future can accommodate many different scenarios and situations, as well as emotional states, for the intention in question. This enables you to face and confront truths in your life, as well as acknowledge how far you have progressed. Examining the past, present, and future helps you recognize patterns and recurring behaviors and find ways to heal what no longer serves you. Tarot presents the opportunity to redirect your current path, based on past actions, to one that better suits your greatest good.

Tarot Offers a New Perspective

Tarot offers the chance to shift your perspective as you read the cards. Many times, we are fixated on what we think we know or the outcome we think we most want. The cards can show us other options or opportunities and alternative ways to view a situation. We are given hidden insight about circumstances to help us better understand what is happening. As we uncover motives, potential outcomes, and deeper emotions, our awareness and perspective begin to shift. Tarot helps us grow, open our mind, and expand our way of thinking.

Tarot Helps Navigate Challenges and Make Decisions

Challenges in life can be difficult to navigate, and sometimes the best decision for ourselves is not always clear. Tarot helps you consider the entirety of a situation, as well as potential outcomes. You are able to explore your feelings, what may be holding you back, and how to overcome obstacles. The cards enable you to uncover and explore the best likely action that aligns with your needs. Sometimes you just need a push from the cards to shed light on how you really feel about a matter or what your intuition has been telling you all along. Tarot lets you sit and think about your challenges, then make choices from a clearer and more grounded space.

Tarot Enhances Self-Expression and Self-Discovery

Reading tarot gives a person a deeper sense of self, offering empowerment through self-discovery and self-expression. Working with the cards enables you to explore your feelings and emotions and uncover parts of you that have been waiting to flourish. Confidence is built, and the cards encourage you to express yourself fully. You may be surprised by what you learn about yourself, your strengths, your desires, and your tenacity! Tarot inspires ideas in readers, as well as action and creativity. Let the cards motivate and guide you to meet a whole new side of you.

Tarot Connects You with Yourself Spiritually and Emotionally

Spiritual and emotional connections are a significant element of tarot practice. The act of tarot reading can be a ritual in itself, and you can deepen that spiritual and emotional connection with your intentions. Many of the tarot cards encourage you to reflect and go within to tap into your intuition and emotions. In doing so, you strengthen both your spiritual and your emotional awareness. Readers can also connect to their spirit guides during readings by setting that specific intention for guidance in order to draw messages from spirit guides and ask for advice.

Tarot Provides Insight into Relationships and Community

Tarot spreads enable you to connect and grow in more harmonious alignment with your relationships and your community. To better understand your role in these relationships, you can set intentions with the cards to explore where each person or group of people is currently resonating in your life. Tarot helps you gain clarity, giving you the tools to heal, grow, and flourish through your connection with others.

Tarot Connects You with Others

Connecting with others through the cards is a special and unique element of tarot. Tarot readings help connect you with others through both exploration with the cards and reading for others. You can learn about your personal connections with others through the cards, allowing meaningful interactions and relationship growth. By reading for other people, such as friends or people in tarot communities, you expand your knowledge and experience. Talking about tarot with other people can be enriching and a learning experience.

Tarot Identifies the Larger Themes and Big Picture of Your Life

Life patterns, themes, and your true calling are all outlined through tarot practice. You are encouraged to follow the purpose that makes you feel most aligned in life, and the cards help you identify that. Tarot offers ways to align your life path so you can live more joyfully and purposefully. Drawing cards can reveal life themes and elements that shape where you have been and where you would most like to end up.

DEALING WITH TABOOS

When you start telling people in your life that you are a tarot reader, you may be met with fear or disapproval from people who don't understand what tarot actually entails. I encourage you to be honest and upfront and always speak your truth. Tarot is not a practice to be ashamed of or to hide away around certain people.

There is a stigma associated with tarot, that it is negative or scary. People often think the cards speak of bad news and prophecies, or that tarot is a dark practice. Explain to your friends and family that we all have free will and the future is not set in stone. The cards are used to give guidance and perspective, not to tell people what to do or what will happen.

While it is important to respect the religious beliefs of others, you can ease the fears of the curious by assuring them that tarot is not bad or an invitation to something creepy. You can explain that tarot is a tool to help people grow, overcome obstacles, and examine situations in their life. There is a spiritual element that enables people to connect to their inner self on a deeper level. Tarot is not evil or dark but rather a practice of self-healing and exploration.

Not everyone will come around to what you do with tarot. However, you will feel more empowered when you stay committed and true to what you do. It's often best not to hide your tarot practice but rather be strong and fearless with the gift you offer.

Tarot Helps You Create and Manifest Goals

Tarot serves as an in-depth tool for putting structure and intention behind achieving your dreams. It can help you create goals that move you toward your visions and manifest what you would like to bring to fruition in your life. You can ask questions to discover the best way to achieve your goals and what steps to take. Journaling about your progress and checking in with the cards helps you stay on track. Draw a card to focus on how to fulfill your intentions. Alternatively, you can choose a card that represents your vision and work with it for manifesting, such as journaling, meditation, or placing it where you can focus on it.

TAROT AND OTHER SPIRITUAL AND HEALING TRADITIONS

Tarot can be used along with both spiritual and healing traditions to offer added support for and deeper insight into those practices. The cards help shed light on areas that need more attention, give messages, or aid with focus during rituals. The cards serve as a guide when working with healing and spiritual elements, suggesting what may need alignment or balance and ways to achieve this.

The cards can also inspire you to focus on your goals, serving as a tool for manifesting them. Tarot assists with intentions and affirmations, reinforcing what you would like to release or bring into your life. If you are using healing or spiritual modalities, tarot can pinpoint what methods to use and the likely outcome, clarify intentions, or offer advice. This can broaden your implementation of healing or spiritual methods, giving you much wider options to explore.

Astrology

Astrology readings that are paired with tarot cards offer additional levels of guidance and under-standing of the area in question. Both astrology and tarot are connected to the elements and planets, and each zodiac sign has associated tarot cards (see page 35). While astrology is more specific and is based in mathematics, the mystical element of the tarot cards balances the reading. Earthly events and planetary positions are rooted in astrology, so when you are doing a tarot reading, the corresponding astrological meanings offer further information to consider. At the same time, the astrological element in the tarot cards defines more characteristics of a person's natural traits and emotions, which helps understand the issues at hand.

Kabbalah

The connection between the Jewish mystical practice of kabbalah and tarot offers a way to enhance spirituality and ties to the divine. People use tarot with kabbalah to study esoteric teachings of the kabbalah and for divination. Tarot cards have also been used as a way to discreetly study and learn the Torah during times of religious persecution. The 22 cards of the Major Arcana correspond to the letters of the Hebrew alphabet and the pathways to the Tree of Life. When studying the Torah was discouraged, the tarot cards offered a way to connect to Torah studies. Kabbalistic readings with tarot cards work toward spiritual awakening and soul development, and an understanding of kabbalah can be a tool for deeper study and interpretation of readings.

Witchcraft

Witchcraft and tarot can easily be blended for spell work, rituals, and manifesting. Tarot offers guidance and amplifies intentions when used with witchcraft, and the outcomes of witchcraft rituals can be understood by way of the cards. If you are practicing witchcraft, the tarot cards can help read the likely outcome of spell work as well as what kind of spell to use. Creating a tarot spread to explore spell work offers guidance and structure to witchcraft rituals. Specific cards can also be chosen from the tarot deck for rituals, spells, and affirmations or mantras. The cards are often placed on altars with candles, crystals, and other divination tools during the practice of witchcraft.

Crystals

Crystals can enhance and amplify tarot readings through the different energies they emit, and they can bring positive energy to the session. During a tarot reading, place crystals around the cards to allow the vibrations into your space. Depending on your intention, you may select grounding crystals to absorb negative energy (such as black tourmaline or obsidian), or crystals for positive energy (such as clear quartz or amethyst). Some crystals connect to higher, divine energies, and others help increase intuition. Some readings may benefit from crystals for healing or love energy, such as rose quartz. You may use as many crystals as you would like for a tarot reading, and you can even intuitively select some beforehand. Crystals and specific tarot cards are also ideal for manifesting by placing a selected crystal over the tarot card that represents your desired intention for a period of time.

Chakras

Chakras are points of energy along the body that correspond to well-being and levels of functioning. You can balance and heal your chakras by reading the tarot cards for each chakra (root, sacral, solar plexus, heart, throat, third eye, crown) to see which ones may be blocked or need healing. You can create a tarot spread by drawing seven cards, one for each chakra, to show their current status. You can then ask the cards what can be done to help heal the chakras. For example, perhaps the cards indicate your throat chakra is blocked due to lack of self-expression. You can then ask for advice on healing this, and perhaps the card drawn may suggest working on speaking your truth with confidence.

Meditation

Tarot complements meditation by expanding the practice and giving focus. Meditating with tarot cards has the benefits of healing and connecting spiritually while also allowing you to develop a deeper understanding of the cards. Meditating with tarot cards also enables you to work on manifestation and affirmations using specific cards you have chosen. If you want to get to know the cards better, you can pull a different card each day to sit and meditate with. Set up as you normally would to meditate, and place the card either between your hands, under your pillow, or by your side. For personal growth, you can ask a question and then pull a card to meditate with. This enables you to reflect and go within. You can choose a card for an intention for manifestation to meditate with, as well.

HOW TO SET INTENTIONS

When it is time to set your intention for your tarot reading, there are ways to ensure you set intentions that are clear. Think about the situation you are seeking insight into, and don't rush yourself when forming your questions.

Are you looking for what is holding you back, advice on a situation, clarity on an issue, or how to manifest a goal? Consider your intention and frame your question in an open-ended manner. Do not ask "yes" or "no" questions; rather, ask "how," "what," or "why." Stay open to all the possible interpretations, as opposed to fixating on one outcome. Use follow-up questions to support your intention based on the message received. You can delve deeply into a situation from the strong foundation you created. Here are some examples of strong intentions.

- How can I stay committed to my goals?

- Why am I feeling stuck in my situation?

- What can I do to move forward?

- Where in my life do I need more balance?

- How can I align myself for my greatest good?

- What patterns from my past are affecting my future?

- Why do I feel scared to take the next step?

- How can I invite abundance and joy into my life?

- What do I need to change for a positive outcome?

- Where do I need to place my focus today?

GET CLEAR ON YOUR INTENTIONS

Setting intentions when reading tarot plays a significant role in every reading. Tarot readings are the most accurate and messages received are easier to read and interpret when your intentions are clear, focused, and specific. If your intention for the reading is scattered, vague, or not fully formed, the message may not make sense or may be inaccurate.

Questions that are direct also allow follow-up questions once the cards are pulled. You can delve deeply into a topic by building a foundation with a solid initial intention. The intention you set helps you figure out what it is you are seeking, and carefully constructed questions allow more specific answers.

Taking ownership of your intentions adds empowerment to your readings. You can also structure what kind of spread you use based on the intentions of your reading, and the cards will offer detailed responses to interpret. Asking the right questions makes all the difference in the outcome of the tarot reading.

THE CARDS CAN POINT YOU IN THE RIGHT DIRECTION

Tarot cards act as a road map, showing you where you currently are in life, what is behind you, and the various routes you can take to get to your destination. They help you assess a situation and then plan how to best proceed for your greatest good. Readings give insight into the bigger picture of the matter at hand and the possible outcomes, depending on which path you choose. The cards can add structure and a foundation for a starting point, guiding you and encouraging you along the way.

Readings may also provide reassurance and validation when you check in, or they may suggest that you shift gears and try a different course. You can discover a general overview of what you may encounter on your journey and the most ideal way to get there.

The Rest Is Up to You

Tarot cards can guide you in the right direction, but the rest is up to you. To achieve your goals and follow your dreams, you alone have to put in the work. The energy of a situation may change, so nothing is ever guaranteed, but following card suggestions helps shift your direction toward a more ideal outcome.

The best way to create change is by taking the necessary steps to do so. Tarot can support you and offer insight, but you are the one who has control of your life. You are the one who decides what to do next. Taking action is the most important step! Without action, the cards merely tell a story. Your efforts are what make the story a possibility.

Now you have become acquainted with tarot, its history, and the basic structure of the deck. The benefits of tarot have been outlined, along with different ways to incorporate reading the cards into your life. With your new insight into the Major and Minor Arcana cards, the suits, and the court cards, you are ready to delve deeper into tarot. In the next chapter you will learn how to connect to your tarot cards, ways to prepare your deck, and tips to enhance your readings. There is also guidance on how to choose the right tarot deck for your needs and how to become more aligned with your deck. You are one step closer to practicing tarot with confidence and ease!

STRENGTH

THE EMPEROR

6 OF WANDS

CHAPTER 3

CONNECTING TO YOUR CARDS AND PREPARING YOUR DECK

BEFORE YOU READ TAROT, IT'S IDEAL to find the right deck for your needs and to clear your deck before working with it and between readings. This chapter will explain how to find the deck that most aligns with you, as well as how to clear this deck by neutralizing or raising its energy between readings and then storing it properly. You will also learn how to strengthen your connection to your cards and ways to enhance your tarot readings. Read on to prepare for a consistent and regular tarot practice, so you can read the cards from a place of informed empowerment.

YOUR TAROT DECK

Your tarot deck is key to unlocking a treasure trove of information. Tarot decks hold so much powerful and transformative energy, with messages to uncover about your life and the world around you. Each card is full of artistic imagery, symbolism, and meaning. All 78 cards work together to unlock a plethora of insight to help you manifest your dreams and strive for personal alignment.

Your tarot deck will be a guide and a familiar source of contemplation. At some point, picking up the cards and shuffling with intent will become second nature. As you lay the cards out before you, so much wonder and possibility waits to be turned over. The artistic design on the back of the cards adds to the energy of the deck, and once you flip the cards, the messages start to flow together. Reading your tarot cards can be an exciting process, and your deck is the key to many explorations and musings.

Choose the Deck That Speaks to You

Choosing the right tarot deck for your practice can be a bit overwhelming with the many decks available today. You may find you have an immediate connection or instinct that a deck is meant for you. If you feel drawn to a certain tarot deck, chances are that deck will be ideal for you to work with. Here are some tips to help you select the tarot deck that speaks to you.

→ Choose a deck with artwork that you are drawn to. There are different themes, color schemes, symbols, and styles, so find a deck whose artwork really resonates with you.

→ Explore different decks to get a feel for card texture, size, and the way the cards feel when you shuffle. This helps you know what type of deck feels comfortable in your hands.

→ Tarot decks have 78 cards in them, so be sure you are purchasing a tarot deck, as opposed to an oracle deck or a nontraditional deck.

→ Many decks have a "little white book" or other reference book that comes with the set and helps you understand the symbolism of those particular cards. If this is important to you, look for a deck that includes a booklet.

→ Find a deck that really speaks to you personally and intuitively. Your deck should feel aligned to you and the way you express yourself.

→ Choose a deck that is suited for your level of experience, such as a more traditional or popular deck for beginners.

THE STANDARD RIDER-WAITE-SMITH DECK

As discussed on page 6, the Rider-Waite-Smith deck is one of the most standard, popular, and influential tarot decks. The structure of the deck and the images on the cards are the foundation for most of the modern decks today. These cards are full of symbolism and vibrant imagery. The Rider-Waite-Smith deck is ideal for beginners, as the cards embody the standard meanings and symbols associated with tarot. While this deck lacks diversity, the foundation it provides makes it a recommended learning tool for beginners.

A MORE INCLUSIVE, MODERN DECK

Many decks have been created today with inclusive artwork that reflects more diversity and contemporary themes. Modern decks are artistic interpretations of tarot using the designer's own vision and theme. These decks still contain the symbolism and elements of tarot while reimagining the standard tarot meanings to fit our very diverse world. Modern decks bring excitement and new perspectives to the card designs, as well as more accessibility to the practice of tarot.

CHOOSE A DECK THAT INCORPORATES THE RIDER-WAITE-SMITH ARCHETYPES

To understand the foundations of tarot, it is important to select a deck that is based on the Rider-Waite-Smith archetypes and interpretations. There are decks that incorporate these standard meanings in updated and more modern versions. Choose a deck that is based on Rider-Waite-Smith to learn the basic principles and fundamental elements of tarot. Once you become more comfortable reading tarot, you may find that your choice of deck expands beyond the traditional structures. For beginner learning and practicing, though, Rider-Waite-Smith decks or modern decks based on Rider-Waite-Smith serve as a solid starting point for learning tarot.

CLEAR AND PURIFY YOUR DECK

Once you choose a new tarot deck, it is important to align with the deck by first clearing its energy. This helps keep positive energy flowing within the cards and promotes clarity in your readings. Here are some ways to clear your deck.

→ Burn herbs, sage, or incense and run the deck through the smoke until it feels energetically lighter. Trust your intuition on this.

→ Wrap the deck in a plastic or paper bag and bury it in a bowl of salt. After a few days remove the deck and dispose of the salt.

→ Place a piece of selenite, clear quartz, or black tourmaline crystal on top of the deck overnight.

→ When the moon is full, place your tarot deck outside or on the windowsill to clear the energy. The same applies to sunlight.

→ Visualize white light around your cards, hold them, and meditate with them for a moment as you imagine the energy lifting away.

→ Shuffle the cards with clearing intentions. Rearrange the cards in order one by one, shuffling to release old energy.

→ Simply knock on the deck a few times with hard, deliberate knocks to shake off the energy.

There is no wrong way to clear your tarot deck. Find the method that resonates best with you!

Store Your Cards in a Safe Place

Tarot cards come in packages that often include a box to store them in. However, there are other ways to store the cards. Many people like to wrap their cards in a silk cloth when not in use. There are also drawstring pouches made specifically for tarot to keep the cards safe and easily accessible. Wooden or ceramic tarot boxes store the cards nicely and protect them quite well. Place your deck in a safe space out of reach of pets and children. To maintain the quality of the deck, it is helpful to read the cards on a soft cloth to preserve their integrity and minimize wear and tear. Washing your hands before handling the deck will help preserve it, too.

HOW I CLEAR THE ENERGY FROM MY TAROT DECK

Tarot decks endure a lot of use, and the energy they contain can feel stagnant. I like to clear my deck before each reading to ensure a fresh start with clear energy for myself or clients. First, I lay down a cloth to place my deck on. A blend of herbs in a seashell is what I most prefer to cleanse my deck with, such as a combination of sustainably harvested white sage, dried lavender, and cedar. I light the herbs, then run my palms through the smoke, as we store energy in our hands to be cleared, as well. I take my deck and run it thoroughly through the smoke, watching the way the smoke wraps around the deck. When the smoke starts to rise smoothly over the deck and I feel intuitively that it is clear, I thank my spirit guides and ask them to make sure the deck is clear and ready to be used again. Then I give the deck a good and vigorous shuffle with the intention of clearing to prepare for the next tarot reading.

Sometimes, I may bring out a deck I have not used in a while or a deck that has been heavily used or has been through some emotional readings. In those instances, I like to clear the deck as I've just described and then leave it with a piece of selenite on the windowsill to absorb sunlight and moonlight for a few days and nights, to remove any prior associations or energies.

STRENGTHEN YOUR CONNECTION TO YOUR CARDS

There are ways to strengthen your connection to your cards to help you be more aligned with the deck and your interpretation of the messages. When you first choose your new deck, set aside some quiet time to connect with your cards. Set up a designated space and sit with the cards. Examine each one, making note of the cards that stand out to you. Observe the images, the symbols, and the feeling the cards evoke. If you journal your tarot experience, jot down key words and any thoughts that arise in connection with the cards that stand out to you. Allow your intuition to guide you as you view the deck. Once you are familiar with the cards, clear the energy as mentioned earlier.

You can express gratitude for the deck and state your intentions for working with it. Another way to connect with your tarot deck is by interviewing the cards to receive an overview of the deck's tone. You may ask questions such as "What can you teach me?" or "What are your strengths?" and "What can you tell me about you?" Then pull a card for each question to better understand the feel of your new deck.

CREATING A SACRED RITUAL

Treating the time you spend with your tarot cards as a sacred ritual helps make readings more consistent. Your space should feel dedicated and special, allowing a more effective interpretation of the cards. Interacting with your cards in a peaceful, nurturing environment is conducive to a stronger, more intuitive connection during readings.

Find a quiet space where you are not likely to be interrupted. Let this be your designated space, and arrange the area to your liking. Decorate the environment to make it peaceful and welcoming, so you can relax and further deepen your insights into the reading.

Additional Items Can Enhance Your Practice

You can enhance your tarot sessions by incorporating different elements into the space you create to practice your readings. Your space should bring a unique and special energy to allow a peaceful state of mind during readings. Think about what makes you feel calm, peaceful, and connected to your intuition, and invite those things into your tarot space. You can place spiritual or meaningful objects that are significant to you in your space, along with candles, essential oils, and incense to create the mood you seek. Many people enjoy the benefits of incorporating crystals into their readings or adding meditative and relaxing music. You can set up an altar in your space, as well. You may want to keep a journal in your space for reflection and further learning about the cards. Any items or elements that you feel would enhance your tarot reading are encouraged.

INCENSE AND CANDLES

Incense and candles add a special ambiance to your tarot reading space. Choose your candles with intention, as different colors represent different kinds of energy. You can select a candle with a color that corresponds to the intention of the reading, such as purple for intuition, white for purity, or black for protection.

Incense, herbs (such as dried rosebuds, lavender, or sage), or cedar can be burned in your space during readings. Clay bowls or abalone shells are ideal vessels for burning herbs. You can fan the smoke around, including over your hands, to clear the energy and calm the atmosphere. You can also use essential oils to add to your practice, either by diffusing them or by placing a few drops of your chosen oil on a cloth or a piece of cotton.

HOW TO USE A JOURNAL TO RECORD AND REFLECT ON YOUR TAROT PRACTICE

Whether you are a beginner or an advanced reader, journaling your tarot experience helps develop your skills. Recording your readings gives you a reference to look back on and offers guidance when you need further insight. Create key words for the cards to write down as a way to trigger your memory of each card meaning. (You will also find key words for each card in part 2.)

Use your journal to record daily card draws, tarot spreads, and reflections on the card meanings. Contemplate readings and observe your interpretations in your journal. For a thought-provoking prompt, find the card in the deck that currently signifies you and write about it. Notice how this changes over time, and record the cards you transition to along the way. Get creative and resourceful with your tarot journal! The more you put into it, the more you'll get out of it.

CRYSTALS

Crystals enhance tarot readings with the different energetic vibrations they emit (see page 18). Pair different crystals with your intentions to amplify the energy of your space. Darker crystals tend to have a protective energy, absorbing or deflecting negative and low vibrations. They also contain grounding properties for support during intense readings. These can include black obsidian, black tourmaline, and shungite. Lighter crystals increase the positive energy and raise the vibration, as well as enhancing intuition. Clear quartz, amethyst, and selenite are good examples. Blue crystals, such as turquoise or aquamarine, encourage expression and truth, while orange and yellow crystals, such as carnelian or citrine, add vitality, confidence, or creativity to the reading. You can also select your crystals intuitively, based on what you are drawn to for your sacred space.

MUSIC

Should you choose to add them, sound elements can enrich your tarot card practice. Choose music that will not distract your focus but rather allow you to deepen it into a relaxed state. Meditation music offers a mindful blend of sounds to promote a calm and peaceful mood. Relaxing sounds, such as rainstorms, the ocean, or forests, can also be used in your tarot reading space. White noise can tune out distractions, blocking outside noise. You can always opt for silence if music doesn't feel right.

AN ALTAR

Altars can serve as a space of reflection and spiritual connection when you practice tarot. Once you select a space, table, or shelf for your altar, you can adorn it with sacred or symbolic items. You may wish to place a tarot cloth on your altar, as well as candles and incense, herbs, or sage. Essential oils and crystals can also enhance your altar, along with flowers. Symbolic objects that are special to you, such as statues, can sit on your altar, as well. Chosen tarot cards can be propped up here on a stand for reflection. Your altar is a special and sacred place to decorate any way you would like.

A JOURNAL

Journals hold our reflections, thoughts, and inspirations. Journals are a helpful tool to place in your sacred space. You can write ideas and notes as you explore tarot, along with your observations and contemplations of the cards or from the readings. Choose a journal that resonates with you to place in your space during tarot practice. You can plan to write in it regularly, or you can just pick it up when the mood strikes. Your journal can serve as a reference guide while you practice, enabling you to look back at patterns, themes, and key words you have recorded. You can track spreads you have pulled from the cards or created when you are inspired.

COMMIT TO A CONSISTENT PRACTICE

Commit to a consistent tarot practice to grow your knowledge of tarot and your confidence in reading the cards. Regular practice expands your understanding of tarot and strengthens your connection to the cards. The more you read, the more experience you gain, building a strong foundation for and relationship to tarot.

Set aside a certain amount of time each week to spend working with your cards. This helps you build consistency, as well as giving you a ritual to look forward to. Ask regular questions, such as a daily card draw or a weekly check-in, to observe patterns over time. You could ask, "What do I need to work on today?" or "What is the energy of this week?" Create a ritual with your tarot practice.

Don't get discouraged if you have moments of frustration or confusion. Take a step back, contemplate, reshuffle the cards, and try again. Consistent and regular interactions with your tarot deck help you grow as a confident reader.

Over time, you will build a relationship of trust and respect with your cards. Working regularly with your cards enables you to expand and strengthen your intuition. You will come to trust your instinct and go with your first impression, allowing the meanings in your readings to flow naturally. Have confidence in yourself and practice regularly. Treat your readings respectfully and with purpose. Being mindful and focused allows you to stay centered and grounded so that trust can develop. In time, you will notice a deeper bond and connection with your tarot cards.

There is so much more to tarot than just choosing a tarot deck and beginning to read the cards. With many decks to choose from, you now have the information to help you select the best deck for your needs. Clearing your deck and preparing your space will be an important part of your tarot ritual, so choose what you are naturally inclined and drawn to for enhancing your environment. Allow yourself to connect with your deck and become more familiar with the practice. Create consistency and build a relationship with your deck, and you'll find tarot has so many benefits to offer. The next chapter will teach you how to effectively read tarot cards so you can practice with confidence.

CHAPTER 4

READING THE CARDS

LEARNING TO READ TAROT TAKES PRACTICE and dedication. But, as with all skills, you start with the basics. In this chapter we'll examine how to connect to your cards and understand their symbolism. You will discover the various aspects of the card imagery and different ways to interpret the cards. You'll learn how to prepare your deck for a reading and how to read for yourself and others. After finishing this section of the book, you will be ready to read tarot. Let's start exploring your tarot cards!

READING TAROT CARDS TAKES PRACTICE

To read with ease and confidence, it is important to commit time to learning tarot. Regular practice enables you to build familiarity and understanding. The cards each have their own meanings, which we will explore in depth in part 2, and as you spend time reading, you will also start to add your own interpretations to each card. You will notice patterns that arise and see how the placement of the cards in a spread affects the message. Your intuition will start to increase as you work with your tarot deck, allowing the readings to eventually become second nature.

As you commit to working with your tarot deck, you will start to see how interpretations come together for you. Tarot is a very layered and deeply symbolic art of self-exploration. The readings, and your depth of intuition, are based on how much you commit to examining the cards and learning their many attributes. The goal is to become more comfortable reading tarot, allowing the messages to come to you naturally and with self-assurance. Consistent practice will help you grow as a reliable and confident tarot reader.

Learning tarot is a dedicated process of exploring and practicing, so be patient with yourself while studying how to read tarot. You will find that you learn and grow alongside the cards, developing into a confident and empowered reader.

Do not get discouraged. When you feel frustrated or the cards you draw don't make sense, take a moment to regroup. Step away and reflect on the reading later. Your mood can affect the outcome of a reading, so come back to the cards again when you are feeling calm and relaxed. You can always clear the cards, shuffle, and pull them again to regain perspective. Go easy on yourself; keep it simple and have fun!

WAYS TO CONNECT WITH THE CARDS

Connecting with your cards helps create alignment with the deck, allowing more effortless and effective reading and increased intuition. There are various ways to connect with the cards; you can start by examining each card in the deck to become familiar with the images and symbols—which are explained in the sections that follow and also in part 2.

Practice becoming familiar with the court cards, the four suits, and the Major Arcana. Notice how they differ and in what ways they are similar. Observe the colors, the themes, the people on the cards. Challenge yourself to apply numerology and symbolism more mindfully as you try out different spreads.

Consistently spend time reading for yourself, as well. Choose a card each day to read or ask a range of different questions. You can keep your intentions serious, or you can practice with lighter inquiries such as "What outfit should I wear today?" or "What kind of book should I read?" to explore all kinds of scenarios with the cards.

Use a journal to track key words that come to mind for each card and for different spreads you use and the questions you ask. Write down your interpretations so you can reflect on them and use your journal entries as a reference tool. You can even meditate with the cards as another way to connect with your deck.

SYMBOLISM IN THE TAROT CARDS

Symbolism plays a large role in the meanings of the tarot cards. The cards are full of symbolic imagery—visual suggestions that imply various emotions, ideas, or mindsets. Symbolism in tarot often takes the form of repeating images, colors, and numbers, the elements, and the zodiac. Animals, bodies of water, and the moon are examples of common symbols found on tarot cards. You'll also encounter doorways, arches, the infinity symbol, lizards, crowns, roses, and trees throughout the cards.

When you are reading the cards, symbols have a foundational meaning, but it is up to you to decide the interpretation based on what the imagery means to you. Reading symbols can enhance and enrich the messages and bring out much more detail.

Christian Mythology

The tarot cards are full of Christian mythological symbolism to enhance the meaning of the message, most notably in the form of angels. Banners reminiscent of the victory of Christ are used to show symbolic triumph, while bells are used to express higher powers and joyful expressions. Circles are used with spiritual connotations and to signify eternity. Christian symbols in tarot also include keys, fish, and doves.

Kabbalah

The kabbalah is referenced in tarot card imagery, particularly with illustrations of the Torah. The theme of balancing masculine and feminine energy, an aspect of kabbalah, is shown throughout the tarot cards. Universal elements of the kabbalah, such as the moon, are also prevalent, and the cards can correlate to the kabbalah's Tree of Life, particularly within the Major Arcana.

Greek Mythology

Greek mythology appears in tarot in many forms, such as the chimera, a creature made up of three animals. There are also references to intertwined snakes, known in Greek mythology as the caduceus. Other images show the Greek rod of Asclepius. Many of the ancient Greek symbols on the tarot cards depict messengers, peace, and the duality of nature.

Egyptian Mythology

Egyptian mythology is portrayed through the Egyptian god Anubis, a jackal-like figure associated with fate. There are also depictions of the sphinx, symbolizing divinity. These elements are connected to the ancient Egyptian god of wisdom, offering mystical and divine options for interpretation. The ankh also appears in tarot, symbolizing life and fertility.

Numerology

Studying the numbers on the Minor Arcana cards helps enhance and amplify your tarot readings. When connecting to your cards, take notice of the numbers that appear during each reading. You may observe patterns, repetitive numbers, or numbers that go in ascending or descending order. This indicates where a person may be in their journey, where they are headed, or what the overall theme may be. Numbers less than five are early stages of a journey, and those greater than five work their way toward completion.

Each number has a specific numerological meaning that has been applied in numerology since ancient times. As you start to learn the meanings of each number, it is a good idea to journal the key words or make a mental note of them to apply during your readings. Once you start to notice the patterns of the card numbers and the associated meanings, you may find your messages are elevated and even more significant. Here's a breakdown of what the numbers mean.

→ **One: New beginnings, possibilities**

→ **Two: Balance, duality**

→ **Three: Growth, creation**

→ **Four: Foundation, stability**

→ **Five: Change, conflict**

→ **Six: Harmony, union**

→ **Seven: Reflection, progress**

→ **Eight: Achievement, action**

→ **Nine: Fulfillment, satisfaction**

→ **Ten: Completion, closure**

The Elements

The four elements—air, water, fire, earth—correspond to the four suits in tarot and show us the energy or attributes of a person and situation during a reading.

→ **Swords** represent **air** and our thoughts, logic, and mental attributes. Often, Swords depict challenges, decisions, or conflict. The suit of Swords has an energy of power and knowledge.

→ **Cups** signify **water**, portraying emotions and feelings, as well as love, relationships, and creativity. The suit of Cups has an intuitive and feminine energy.

→ **Wands** relate to **fire** and passion, showing us action, goals, inspiration, and spirituality. The suit of Wands holds an empowering and masculine energy.

→ **Pentacles** symbolize **earth** and material possessions, such as health, career, and finances. The suit of Pentacles brings grounding, stabilizing energy, and manifestation.

Colors

Colors have symbolic meanings on tarot cards, often correlating to the colors of chakras to give us an understanding of the energy suggested by the cards.

→ **Black** and **red** relate to the root chakra, indicating security and being grounded.

→ **Orange** relates to the sacral chakra, showing passion and creativity.

→ **Yellow** connects to the solar plexus chakra, with empowerment and confidence.

→ **Green** signifies the heart chakra, with love and compassion.

→ **Blue** indicates expression and truth, relating to the throat chakra.

HOW THE MOON AFFECTS YOUR TAROT PRACTICE

The phases of the moon can enhance your tarot readings if you create spreads that work with the energy that's present at the time. Each phase of the moon represents a different place in our own cycles of personal change and growth. During certain phases of the moon, I like to draw cards about how I can make the most of the moon's energy at that time. The moon's phases can serve as a check-in point for personal development, supported by the guidance of the tarot cards.

For the **new moon**, use the tarot cards to reflect on new beginnings and reassess where you currently are in life or with your goals. Think about where you would like to be, and use this as a new starting point.

When the **waxing moon** arrives, read the cards for ways to examine already existing foundations or obstacles in your life and how you would like to proceed. For example, are you happy in your career? Would you like to advance? What steps can you take?

The **full moon** places emphasis on spirituality, intuition, and personal growth. This is a time to appreciate your gains and be grateful for all you have. Use your tarot cards to explore what you would like to manifest and bring to fruition in your life.

For the **waning moon**, draw cards about what you need to release that no longer serves you. Examine what you can let go and what needs to be nurtured.

→ **Purple** or **violet** correlates to the third eye, showing intuition and spirituality.

→ **White** suggests purity and divinity, connecting to the crown chakra.
  You can also use your own associations with different colors when interpreting meanings.

The Zodiac

Incorporating astrological elements into tarot can offer further insight into your readings by giving more depth and understanding of a person's traits and characteristics. Astrological signs correspond to some cards in the Major Arcana (see part 2), and the elements of the suits in the Minor Arcana also represent the different astrological signs.

→ **Cups (water)** are related to Cancer, Scorpio, and Pisces.

→ **Wands (fire)** are related to Leo, Aries, and Sagittarius.

→ **Pentacles (earth)** are related to Taurus, Virgo, and Capricorn.

→ **Swords (air)** are related to Gemini, Libra, and Aquarius.

CLEAR YOUR MIND BEFORE YOU DO A READING

Clearing your mind before you do a tarot reading for yourself or others allows you to read from a more centered and grounded place. When we quiet our minds and bring ourselves to a more relaxed state, we release expectations and allow the information to flow to us with ease.

Before reading, set up your space so that it feels peaceful. Remove any distractions, such as cell phones. You may light candles to soften the atmosphere, gather crystals to complement the energy, or light some incense, diffuse oils, or burn herbs. You may play soothing music if it helps you clear your mind in preparation for the reading. I like to place rose oil over my third eye to raise my vibration before readings.

Allow yourself to deepen into a more relaxed state. Sit for a moment, close your eyes, and focus on your breath. Focus on your thoughts, and allow them to roll away as you breathe in and out. Repeat a mantra or affirmation if necessary to center yourself, such as "With every breath I feel more calm" or "I quiet my mind and embrace peace." When your mind feels relaxed and clear, you are ready to start the tarot reading!

PREPARE YOUR DECK

When you are ready to read the cards, it is important to prepare your deck. This helps you connect to the cards and clear the energy of the deck for a reading. Think of it as a clean slate or a fresh start before a reading, wiping away any residual energy so the deck is free of previous impressions that may affect the message.

For new decks or one you have not used in a while, take some time to look through the cards to become familiar with them. Observe how they make you feel and any cards that stand out to you. Clear your deck with crystals, sound, moonlight, smoke, or salt. For instance, you can burn some herbs or incense and run the tarot cards through the smoke until the deck feels energetically lighter. If you need a refresher on how to clear your deck, see page 25. Once the deck has been prepared, you are ready to start reading.

ASK THE CARDS A QUESTION

Now it's time to ask the cards a question! The way you formulate your tarot questions can make the difference between a good reading and a confusing one. Get clear with yourself on your intentions and what you would like to explore. Questions should always be open-ended, such as how, what, or why.

Avoid yes-or-no questions in a tarot reading, as this limits the insight being offered. For example, instead of asking, "Will I find my ideal spouse?" try asking, "What is the best way to find my ideal spouse?" This opens up a wide range of information to examine with the cards, and it also allows follow-up questions.

Here's another example: Instead of "Will I be promoted at work?" ask, "Why haven't I been promoted at work yet?" to explore the reasons and obstacles to overcome. Use your questions to make the most of your tarot reading, receiving richer and deeper messages from the cards.

SHUFFLE THE CARDS

Shuffling tarot cards before a reading realigns the energy and connects you to the cards. Focusing on a question while shuffling helps reinforce the intentions of the reading. So how do you shuffle the cards? There is no wrong way to shuffle your tarot cards! Find a method that works for you.

You can shuffle overhand by taking a portion of the deck from the front and bringing it around and behind the section you are holding, repeating this with different sections until the deck feels shuffled enough. There is the old-fashioned shuffling method of splitting the deck in half and weaving the cards together as you fan them in each hand. Another option is to cut the tarot deck into as many piles as you prefer and stack them on top of one another to shuffle the cards. Fanning out the cards on the table in front of you and mixing them around until you pull them back into a pile also shuffles the cards.

When you shuffle before a reading, any cards that jump out can be placed aside and incorporated into the reading. To pull cards, choose the ones you are drawn to without overthinking it. You can pull at random, cut the deck, choose the cards on the top . . . whatever cards you pick are the cards you were meant to choose.

HOW TO READ THE CARDS

When you read the tarot cards, remember to keep it simple and to have fun. Focus on your intention and choose a spread that best suits your needs. Shuffle the cards with your question in mind and lay them facedown in the pattern of the spread. Now it is time to read the cards!

Flip them over one by one and examine the images. What are you immediately drawn to? What is your first thought? Look further and observe the symbols on the cards, as well as the colors. What feeling is evoked? Is it a court card? A Major Arcana? Notice what element the suit is associated with. Read the numbers of each card and contemplate the additional meaning. Observe the placement of the cards and the order in which they appear, and you can start to put together the story that's in front of you.

Now use what you know and what you feel to answer your question. Let your intuition guide you. Reflect on the message you have interpreted. You may record the reading in your journal for reference. You have just done a tarot reading!

REVERSALS

Reading a reversal can bring added insight to the message. Reversals occur when a card ends up upside-down as opposed to upright when you turn it over. Based on the context of the surrounding cards, the imagery, and your intuition, you can read the reversals naturally, as you normally would read the tarot cards, or you can explore the reversed meaning of the card—it's a personal choice for the reader. Some readers always read reversals, and others do so when they feel drawn to, while some never do.

Reversed tarot cards can have different meanings, and it is ultimately up to you to interpret how you read them based on your intuition and the context. At times, reversals can depict the meaning of the tarot card, just to a lesser degree or with a temporary setback. For example, The Sun reversed can indicate success and happy outcomes are still likely, just delayed or to a lesser extent than originally expected. Often, reversed cards may show the internal energy of the querent (the person you are reading for), a blockage in a situation, imbalanced energy, or a delay. (See part 2 for more about the meanings of reversals.)

When reading reversals, it is helpful to read the imagery and symbolism in the upside-down position to gain a better sense of the meaning. In this position you are able to read the cards from a different perspective. You can enhance your tarot reading skills by practicing reading reversals to open up a whole new avenue of possibilities and meanings.

HOW TO READ FOR YOURSELF

When you are familiar with the tarot cards and acquainted with your deck, it is time to start reading for yourself. Think about your intention: Are you seeking practical guidance for everyday situations or deeper exploration of a more spiritual or personal nature? Once you know what you would like to examine, choose a specific and open-ended question. Decide on a spread or pattern in which you would like to draw the cards. (See chapter 5 for more information on tarot spreads.) For example, you might draw two cards for an obstacle and advice to overcome it, or three cards for a past, present, and future spread. Have your journal ready to make notes during the reading. Some people like to say a mantra or a prayer or ask their spirit guides for guidance before they start.

Shuffle your cards, and then start pulling the ones you are drawn to and placing them face-down in your chosen spread pattern. When you are ready, turn them faceup. Observe the cards and allow them to tell you a story. Let the interpretations flow naturally as you notice the images, the symbolism, the numbers, and the order the cards are placed in. (If you're unsure what a card means, refer to the card profiles in part 2.)

Now answer your question based on the message you are reading. Reflect on the message and record your observations. If you feel you need more information, you may ask a follow-up question and draw the relevant number of cards. You have now read tarot for yourself!

The Pros and Cons of Reading for Yourself

Reading tarot for yourself allows you to really connect with the cards and learn how to practice tarot. It increases your intuition, strengthens your skills, and enhances your personal development. It offers a chance for regular practice and incorporating spiritual rituals into your life.

However, reading for yourself can also cause confusion when you are too attached to an outcome or too close to a situation. You may not expect the message that comes up, or it may not make sense because you had your mind and hopes already strongly set on one outcome. When someone reads for you, they are coming from a more neutral and observant place. A healthy balance of reading for yourself and holding awareness of potential bias is encouraged and recommended.

HOW TO READ FOR OTHERS

Prepare your space to promote a relaxing environment, even if you are performing the reading remotely or from a distance. Approach the session from a calm and confident place to ensure clear interpretations. Talk to your querent (the person you are reading for) to understand their intentions. Form a question together, and choose a spread to best answer the inquiry and provide clarity. Keep it simple and don't overthink.

After clearing your deck, shuffle the cards when you are ready, focusing on the designated intention. Some readers like to say a mental prayer or a mantra of good intentions before starting. Follow your instinct about whether this feels right for you. Pick up the cards you are drawn to and place them facedown in your chosen spread.

Turn over the cards that you have drawn and start to process the information as it comes to you, noticing anything that stands out. When you are ready, start to deliver the message. Always approach your querent with tact and honesty. Do not hide information that may be unpleasant; rather, deliver it in an open and respectful manner. Allow the querent to give feedback or ask follow-up questions.

If you need more information to understand a card that was drawn or to answer a follow-up question, you can pull another card, asking for clarity without having to create a new spread. Shuffle and draw more cards as needed to answer and provide further clarification. Once you have completed the reading, end from a place of gratitude and clear your cards.

A SAMPLE READING

Drawing one card daily helps you connect to your cards and learn their meanings, while also offering inspiration and personal growth. Whether you are reading for yourself or a querent, drawing a single card offers clarity and the opportunity to strengthen your intuition. A one-card pull eliminates clarifying cards, encouraging you to honor your instinct as you read the message.

In this sample reading we will ask, "What is the best way to take care of myself today?" Shuffle your cards with this intention and pull the card you feel drawn to. Here we have pulled the Eight of Wands.

8 OF WANDS

Notice the wands pointing forward, with green leaves blooming from them. They speak of urgency and transformation as they fly through the air. The orange-yellow color suggests empowerment, creativity, and inspiration. The blue water suggests perspective, abundance, flow, and growth. There is an element of freedom and expression, and we see change at a quick pace. We can interpret the message this way:

Change is unfolding rapidly, so keep moving forward. Go with the flow of the energy and surrender the need for control. Stay focused on your vision and don't give up. Your ideas are coming to fruition, so allow your passion to propel you forward. Keep going, stay focused, and allow change to flow naturally today.

One-card spreads are simple to pull and allow you to stretch your intuition and observations of the cards. There are many other kinds of spreads to create and explore, giving more structure and clarity to your readings. Tarot spreads help you focus on your intention and create patterns that offer detailed messages in response to your questions. We will discuss and delve further into tarot spreads in chapter 5.

HOW TO CLOSE A READING

Tarot readings can have a lot of energy connected to the session. It is recommended to close the reading in a manner that signifies that the session is over and clears yourself and your space. When you are certain you or your querent feel the reading is sufficient, you may express gratitude to the person for choosing to read with you. When reading for yourself, you may give thanks to the cards, your spirit guides, or any other source you feel inclined to acknowledge as having provided support or guidance. You may say a prayer asking to clear the energy from the reading. Burning herbs, incense, or sage will also clear the energy and intentionally mark the closing of the reading.

Taking these measures helps protect your energy and ground yourself after the reading. Any other methods that resonate with you are encouraged, such as spraying a blend of soothing essential oils in the air or visualizing yourself surrounded by white light. Closing a tarot reading allows your mind to shift from the energy and intensity of the session, signaling completion until next time.

REMEMBER, LEARNING TAROT TAKES TIME

Learning the art of tarot takes time. There are 78 cards to become familiar with, and each card is full of symbolism and meaning. Different questions and spreads offer a variety of possibilities to explore, and each time you read the cards the interpretations may vary, depending on the scenario.

Regular practice helps you build a strong foundation of tarot knowledge. Practice reading for yourself, your friends, your family, fictional characters, and even your pets! Not every reading has to be super serious. Try different spreads and switch up the kinds of questions you ask the cards. Journal the sessions, your observations, and key words to reference. Draw cards daily to connect and become more familiar with the deck. Over time you will notice patterns and start to recognize the card meanings. The more comfortable and confident you become, the more easily the information will start to flow to you.

Release Any Fear or Doubt

Whether you are new to tarot or a seasoned reader, there may be moments when you doubt your intuition or lack confidence during a reading. It is important to release any fear or doubt you have when doing tarot readings. Remember that you already know the cards. Trust your intuition! Your first thought is usually the right thought, so go with your instinct.

What may not make sense to you will likely resonate with your querent as you read, so don't be afraid or hold back your message because you are unsure. Read with confidence and certainty, allowing a natural flow. You will be surprised at how the readings relate and give clarity, even if you feel unsure at first. Go in feeling empowered and don't hesitate to share your message.

As you study and learn to work with the cards, you will rely more on your intuition to interpret the meanings of each reading. The messages will flow to you more naturally as you learn to trust yourself and your inner knowing. Your confidence will increase, and you will honor your intuition as you read tarot, feeling more mindful and empowered.

Don't Start by Looking for a Specific Answer

When reading tarot, especially for yourself, do not go into the reading expecting a specific answer. Read the cards objectively and intuitively and be receptive to the information you receive. Embrace what comes through and use this as a tool to help you align with what resonates for your best interest. Ultimately, you are the one who has control of your life, and nothing is ever set in stone. Reflect on the message and on how to shift the energy if the outcome drawn is unexpected. Tarot readings are full of possibilities, opportunity, and insight, so allow yourself to go with the flow of whatever message the cards bring your way.

Open Yourself Up to the Wisdom of the Cards

Tarot cards are full of guidance, advice, and wisdom. The key to experiencing the wisdom of the cards is to open yourself up. The insight received from readings can help overcome obstacles and bring dreams to fruition. Go into the readings with an open mind and without expectations or attachments to outcomes. Allow yourself to receive the messages and reflect on their meanings.

We tap into our inner knowing and our intuition when we practice tarot, so it is important to trust your instinct. While you should never go against your beliefs or take actions that do not resonate with you, there is much to be learned from the wisdom of the tarot cards. Keep an open mind and embrace the art of tarot.

As you reflect on interpretations and the actions you may have taken based on your readings, you will start to notice the ways in which advice from the cards influenced situations in your life. Recognizing your own behavior and emotions through tarot reading will help shift you into a more aligned state of being. Over the course of time, learning tarot can support a harmonious bond between you, the cards, and the lessons you learn as you practice reading.

4 OF CUPS   QUEEN OF PENTACLES   KING OF SWORDS   4 OF SWORDS   KNIGHT OF CUPS

CHAPTER 5

SAMPLE TAROT SPREADS AND READINGS

A SINGLE TAROT CARD HOLDS A wealth of information, but a spread offers even more insight. A tarot spread is a predetermined pattern for placing the cards you've chosen that corresponds to certain aspects of your question. Spreads play a significant role in tarot by setting a clear guide to follow when you read the cards. They are a great way to see everything you need to know in one reading and are an important part of reading for yourself and others.

In this chapter you will learn the importance of tarot spreads and how they can help your readings. You'll learn how to set up and prepare spreads so that you can use them comfortably. You will see examples of different spreads you can use and how they might work to enhance your readings. When you are able to prepare a tarot spread, your practice will start to open more fully and offer more possibilities to explore. Let's start creating some tarot spreads!

SEEING THE BIGGER PICTURE

A tarot spread enables the cards you pull to tell a full story, giving you a much broader view. Spreads provide a detailed structure to work from that offers comprehensive guidance for the questions at hand, because each card represents a specific part of the reading. Each card is assigned a meaning or role in your spread, and when you flip them over, the message unfolds following the pattern you have created. This provides a framework within which to interpret the story.

For example, you might explore your career by setting up a spread to highlight how things have been going, where they are now, the likely future of your career, and advice to advance further. This can all be encompassed in one reading when you work with a spread. Using the meaning of the cards, along with your intuition, you are able to weave together an engaging story as you delve deeply into the question.

The Position of the Cards Tells the Story

The position of the cards in a tarot spread is an important part of the interpretation. When creating a tarot spread, position the cards to tell a clear story. Lay out the spread in a pattern that will allow the message to flow freely and avoid confusion as you read the message. A common tarot spread is past, present, future (see page 49). The layout very clearly expresses the meaning of each card—which offers much more detail than the individual cards alone would convey. You are given a better idea of scenarios, with each card clearly representing aspects of the question that need more understanding.

START WITH A TWO-CARD SPREAD AND GO FROM THERE

Learning tarot spreads can be overwhelming at first, when you are still new to the cards. Keep it simple at the beginning; start small and expand slowly. You are already familiar with pulling a daily card to reflect on, so now start reading a two-card spread and work your way up from there.

Use the two-card spread for any situation you would like—the meaning of the spread can be flexible, depending on your question. Try using a "this or that" approach with the cards, thinking of a choice you are trying to make. Pull a card for each option and interpret the advice in your spread. You can use easy issues, like what to make for dinner, or delve into something serious. Strength/ weakness, now/later, and do/don't are other ideas you can work with for two-card spreads. This practice will help you become familiar working with spreads and allow you to be more comfortable as you progress to spreads with more cards.

To avoid confusion, you may want to wait until you feel comfortable with simpler spreads before working with advanced spreads. Once you become familiar with asking clear questions and choosing the right spread and setup for your reading, more complex spreads will be easier to incorporate into your practice. As you examine the cards in front of you regularly, advanced spreads will start to resonate with your intentions to offer more in-depth information and a wider range of areas to cover.

JUMPER, SHADOW, AND CLARIFIER CARDS

Sometimes other cards can be acknowledged during a reading. These options are all personal preferences, so work only with what resonates.

When you have chosen your tarot spread, a card may jump out while you are shuffling. You can either put this **jumper card** back in the deck, use it as the next designated card, or set it to the side to incorporate into the message. Use your intuition as to how this card flows into the reading, usually highlighting the answer to your question.

The **shadow card** is the card at the bottom of the deck. There are readers who, after laying out their spread and reading over the cards, will pick up the deck to see what card is waiting on the bottom. This card often signifies the underlying or hidden energy of the reading and can be incorporated into the overall message. The shadow card can bring issues to the surface that revolve around your question, or it can give more insight into the theme.

Clarifier cards can be used while reading a spread to shed light on a card whose meaning feels too vague to interpret. Once the cards have been drawn, if there is a card that needs more explanation, you can pull a clarifier card for more context. Be mindful not to pull too many clarifiers, as this can lead to feeling overwhelmed and confused. Try working first with the cards in the original spread, and resort to clarifiers only when you truly feel you need more clarity and context.

HOW TO SET UP AND INTERPRET SPREADS

Create a tarot spread by formulating a clear question based on an understanding of your goal or intention. Many readings explore the circumstances of a situation, the underlying obstacles, and the solution. You may use one of the spreads explained in this chapter or another one from a trusted tarot resource, or you may create a spread of your own. Put thought into your question and into what will be the best spread to answer it.

Once you know the layout of your desired spread, shuffle with intention. Place the cards in the pattern with careful thought to ensure an insightful and coherent reading. When you are ready to read, flip them over. Examine the cards, weaving a story that answers your questions. Use your intuition and combine it with your knowledge of tarot.

Each card offers its own meaning to the reading, and as part of a spread each card influences the entire tarot message. Observe the interactions between the cards and how they complement one another to tell your story. Notice the themes and common occurrences that stand out among the cards, such as the colors, numbers, and symbols. Integrate them into the story, allowing your message from the spread to flow naturally.

Notice the placement of the cards. Pay attention to the position of the characters and observe the direction they are facing in relation to one another. Perhaps the people on the cards are facing each other or face away from each other—this may have relevance to your reading.

Put everything together to answer your question. Take notes in your journal to record what comes to mind. When you have interpreted the message, take a moment to reflect. If you need to ask a follow-up question, go ahead. Close your session when you have finished reading the spread.

FEAR/REALITY SPREAD

This is a two-card spread to help you understand what may be causing you anxiety in a situation, highlighting what you fear and the reality of the situation. Use this to feel more centered and empowered.

1. *Fear* 2. *Reality*

We have pulled Judgement as the card in the fear position. This reveals that you may be feeling worried that you are not living your true calling or following your life purpose. You are faced with several possibilities and may be scared you are not reinventing yourself for your greatest good. The Judgement card is showing there may be some self-doubt as you are nearing the end of a situation and may have some choices to make.

The reality is depicted through the Two of Wands. We see that you actually have made quite a bit of progress, as shown by the world in your hand and the vast landscape before you, with one hand firmly holding a wand and another wand standing at your side. You are being asked to decide which path best suits you. This is a time for self-discovery and a chance to step outside your comfort zone.

You are being asked to fully explore your options before embarking on your next move, so that you align with your calling.

This spread, like many others, can be used for other intentions and questions. The two-card spread offers many options to explore when trying to gain clarity in a situation. Try thinking of other questions for which you can use this two-card spread when trying to make a decision or gain more insight into an issue.

PAST, PRESENT, FUTURE

This classic three-card tarot spread shows the progression of a situation: where you have been, where you are now, and where you are headed. This spread is easily adapted to different intentions.

1. *Past* 2. *Present* 3. *Future*

In this example, we will ask, "What do I need to focus on to bring more harmony to my life?" In this example we have drawn the Ace of Cups in the past position. It seems that in the past acting with compassion and expressing creativity brought you joy. There was an emotional connection to the creativity, allowing a more harmonious flow. We read this from the water, representing emotion and creativity, as it overflows from the cup while the hand breaks through the clouds.

Currently, working and collaborating with others on projects and ideas brings happiness to your life, as shown in the Three of Pentacles. Learning new things from others and implementing techniques to put your ideas into motion are currently bringing more harmony to your life. We are shown this in the card as three people work together on the same project toward a common goal. As we interpret the cards, we can connect the Ace of Cups from the past position and weave it into the same creative theme.

Going forward, the Queen of Pentacles suggests that nurturing yourself will help you feel better attuned. This card advises that you create a balance between work and play and have a loving yet practical approach when tending to your needs. The rabbit, plants, and flowers surrounding the Queen, along with the way she holds and views the pentacle in her hand, show her connection to nature, the flow of life, and her ability to nurture. We are shown through the previous two cards that creating and collaborating are important to you, and here the Queen encourages finding a balance while honoring self-care.

ACE OF PENTACLES

3 OF WANDS

10 OF PENTACLES

7 OF CUPS

ACE OF WANDS

OVERCOMING OBSTACLES

This five-card spread helps you see what obstacle is standing in your way, as well as any hidden influences affecting your situation. Use this for insight on how to overcome a challenge.

1. *Situation* 2. *Obstacle*
3. *Hidden Influences*
4. *Advice for Obstacle*
5. *Advice for Influences*

For this sample, we will ask, "What is preventing me from advancing in my career?" This spread can be adapted to any kind of question, so you may use it for other intentions.

The situation card is the Ace of Pentacles, showing that there is a possibility for a new career opportunity. This new beginning has the potential for success and abundance and is ready to be turned into something tangible. The unexpected hand offering the pentacle from the clouds above a flourishing garden with an archway indicates this new opportunity for prosperity. You have the chance to manifest your dreams.

The obstacle is represented by the Three of Wands. Here we see that there are many potential opportunities being presented to you, and you are being asked to expand your horizons. The ship sailing in open water represents movement forward and a chance to progress further. The sea and mountains in the far distance signify opportunity and a need to assess challenges as you proceed with your plans. Step outside of your comfort zone and realize that there are challenges ahead if you decide to follow this new opportunity.

Hidden influences are reflected in the Ten of Pentacles, depicting the need for security and long-term success. This is a card of establishment, security, and lasting prosperity, which we can see by the older person surrounded by their family and a home adorned with lush gardens. This indicates there may be a conflict between playing it safe to have wealth and stability or following the unknown path to your dreams. That conflict may be holding you back from taking advantage of new opportunities.

The advice card for the obstacle is the Seven of Cups. Overcome this challenge by not getting overwhelmed by the many different choices in your head. You can see that the cups in the clouds are filled with different items, representing the different dreams or wishes you have or your opportunities to choose from. With so much being offered, it becomes challenging to focus on one choice. Instead of overthinking and fantasizing about the possibilities, you are encouraged to act on them.

Your hidden influences can be resolved by taking action on your ideas and inspirations through the Ace of Wands. This card shows you that following your passion and heart has the possibility to be fulfilling and exciting. The hand on the card is holding a budding wand of inspiration while hovering above a fertile landscape with a castle, indicating the possibility of acting on your ideas and inspirations to achieve your dreams. Follow your instinct and jump on the ideas that align with your dreams.

RELATIONSHIP ALIGNMENT SPREAD

This spread works well for any relationship experiencing misalignment, in order to understand where each person is currently and how to shift things back to a more balanced place. The fourth card highlights how you inspire each other.

Here we have drawn the Justice card to reflect you in the first position. This is telling us that you are seeking more fairness and accountability in the relationship, and the truth is important to you. Notice the scale in her hand as she stands between two structured pillars. These symbols indicate a need for balance, and the double-edged sword she holds shows us final decisions and consequences to our actions. You stand by your decisions and beliefs and expect the same kind of fairness and loyalty in return.

The other person in your relationship is signified by the Five of Cups. Look at the figure on the card. This person seems to be feeling disappointed and sad. There is a feeling of sorrow and regret. They may not be appreciating you in the present because they are fixated on upsets from the past. This person may be in a negative mindset, stuck in the past and unable to move forward at the moment. We see this in the card through the spilled cups, while upright ones wait near the person to be noticed.

The World is the card in your realignment position. This is showing you that to have closure and wholeness in your relationship, any loose ties or insecure pieces must be addressed to bring about completeness. We see this through the large laurel wreath, tied together in a circle. The circle shows wholeness and completion when fully enclosed, and the wands signify manifesting your achievements, along with balance from the zodiac symbols. The woman is stepping through the wreath, finishing one journey and ready to start another. Address the issues at hand and find ways to bring back a sense of fulfillment. Seek to enjoy triumph and celebrate successes together.

The Two of Pentacles shows us that you inspire each other by balancing each other out; we see a man balancing and juggling two pentacles wrapped in an infinity symbol as he dances in front of choppy, turbulent waters. This shows the ability to balance for as long as necessary, no matter the circumstances. Together, you complement each other and offer a blend that keeps your relationship in a state of harmony. You each bring parts of yourself that together create an infinite loop of balance, allowing you to adapt to each other's needs.

PERSONAL GROWTH SPREAD

This is a more advanced spread I created to explore your personal growth and get advice on how to live more in alignment with your purpose. This is helpful to check in with yourself and connect more deeply.

This spread explores how your past has influenced you today. The higher self represents yourself without limits, as you were intended to be. You are shown what it is you desire right now and the challenges you are facing. The last two cards show what you need to learn to fall into alignment and advice on how to move forward.

1. *Past Self* 2. *Current Self* 3. *Higher Self*
4. *Desire* 5. *Challenge* 6. *Lesson to Learn*
7. *Advice*

We pulled The Star as the past self, suggesting you had been searching for hope, purpose, or something more to life. We see this through a naked woman under the stars, indicating pureness and vulnerability, with one foot on land and the other in the water, showing her logical and intuitive sides. She balances water in each hand, the subconscious and the conscious. The stars behind her are full of hope, promise, and faith and represent the seven chakras. The bird in flight speaks of higher thoughts and wisdom.

The Nine of Pentacles, the current self, shows us that you have accrued abundance and prosperity. Notice the lush garden in which the well-dressed woman on the tarot card stands. There are grapes, pentacles, and a falcon. This portrays the fruits of her labor, signifying decadence and prosperity. You are independent and financially stable, but have you found your purpose or fulfillment?

The Strength card in the position of the higher self reveals wanting inner strength, perseverance, and confidence. See how she remains calm and graceful as she pets and soothes the ferocious lion. Wearing white robes of purity under an infinity symbol to denote her wisdom, the woman uses her inner strength to tame the beast.

The King of Wands shows that you desire to be a leader, in control of your own destiny and liked by others. The lions and salamanders on the King's robe, throne, and crown represent strength, fire, and passion. The motion of the salamanders symbolizes overcoming challenges, leading, and paving the way no matter what. The King's sprouting wand speaks of ambition and growth as he sits on a throne representing power and leadership.

The challenge is represented by the Five of Wands. You may be comparing yourself to others and feeling envious. You can see the chaos and tension in this card by observing the men with their raised wands. They are causing discontent, yet when you look closely, you see that they have not actually hit each other. This card speaks also of confusion, comparison, and competition, as each person on the card is different. This card suggests you may be causing yourself inner conflict and creating a struggle to get ahead.

We move now to the Seven of Swords as the lesson to be learned. This card suggests that you may be selling yourself short and need to learn how not to cheat yourself out of your true nature and full potential. Observe how the man on the card is sneaking away from a military camp. He holds five swords and looks back at the two he left behind as he smiles with pride over escaping with the swords unnoticed. His actions depict deception, betrayal, cheating or lying, and acting strategically. You are encouraged to learn how to be more honest with yourself and true to your needs.

For advice, we are shown the Knight of Swords. The Knight encourages you to speak your truth from a place of self-assurance and empowerment. The Knight's armor and white horse symbolize the purity and energy of his intelligence, and the sword represents dedication and confidence. You can see the wind blowing the trees through the stormy clouds, as the Knight keeps moving forward without fear or hesitation. Do not hesitate to express yourself with confidence and strength so that you can move into the desired roles of Strength and the King of Wands.

HOW TO CREATE YOUR OWN SPREADS

There are so many tarot spreads to choose from, but sometimes nothing really fits your situation. When that happens, create your own spread. You can design a spread that is specifically tailored to your needs and addresses the entirety of your intention.

To create your own spread, you can base it on an existing spread. Take your situation and alter the questions and format of a spread you have worked with before to encompass your scenario.

You can also create an entirely new spread. Begin by contemplating your intentions. Start working out placements for cards and what each spot represents. Try to allocate one card to explore the situation, one to explain any obstacles, and one to offer advice or solutions. From there, you can incorporate more cards to represent different areas that require insight. Make sure the pattern has a card spot for each area that needs clarity. When you feel confident about the design, shuffle with intention as you normally would and start using your newly created spread. You may want to record your spread in your journal for reference and future use.

STRENGTHEN YOUR SKILLS

To really test your intuition and explore the cards, try an unstructured spread. By that I mean that you start by thinking about the situation or intention you would like clarity on. Shuffle the cards with intent, focusing on your question or area that needs examination. Ask what it is you most need to know about the situation in the moment. When you are ready, pull as many cards as you would like, without a pattern in mind. I usually pull three cards for this technique and line them up in a row. Turn the cards over and read them as they are, allowing your intuition to spark the message. Go where your attention is drawn and quickly start to piece together the message, shedding light on what you most need to know at that moment. This is a good way to strengthen your skills and instincts while also receiving inspiration and guidance.

PART TWO

BRINGING THE CARDS TO LIFE

E very tarot card is different. In part 2 we'll bring the cards to life by breaking down each of the 78 cards to learn about the symbolism, colors, numerology, astrology, elements, and key words associated with each card—whether it's pulled upright or reversed. These key words will help you have a basic understanding of each card's meaning. It's important to remember that every tarot deck, even Rider-Waite-Smith decks, interpret cards differently. Some of the details here may not be found on your cards (or the cards pictured) but occur frequently enough among the many different RWS decks that they're worth mentioning. You'll also get detailed descriptions for some specific intentions, such as love and career advice. The Wild Card category offers additional and alternative interpretations for each card.

As you start to learn the cards, you will begin to incorporate your own meanings into the overall message. There are subtle differences between tarot decks, so this guide may be a little different from the interpretations that come with your deck. But this information will give you a solid foundation to learn from.

CHAPTER 6

THE MAJOR ARCANA

MAJOR ARCANA CARDS DEAL WITH THE major experiences we encounter during the various journeys we embark on in life. These cards revolve around different life lessons, themes, and influences. Collectively, these 22 cards are archetypes that depict a person's life journey from the very beginning to the end—what's known as The Fool's Journey. The Fool card starts the journey, reflecting new beginnings and optimism. The World depicts the end of the adventure, the last card of The Fool's Journey.

THE FOOL

THE FOOL

NUMEROLOGY: Innocence

ASTROLOGY: Uranus

ELEMENT: Air

COLORS: White, Yellow, Blue, Green, Orange

SYMBOLS: Rose, Dog, Cliff, Mountains, Knapsack

UPRIGHT KEY WORDS: Innocence, New Beginnings, Leap of Faith, Carefree

Upright Meaning

The Fool speaks of new beginnings and embarking on a new journey. The card suggests opportunities and has a feeling of innocence. The Fool is carefree and ready to jump into a new situation with confidence that everything will work out. There is a feeling of excitement and curiosity. The Fool embraces the unknown and acts spontaneously, playfully, and without fear. There is a youthful element and a sense of freedom to this card.

REVERSED KEY WORDS: Reserved, Irresponsible, Cautious, Impulsive, Risky

Reversed Meaning

The Fool reversed can indicate a lack of preparation or not being ready when it comes to new plans. There may be a fear of the unknown or a feeling of being held back. This card can show reckless behavior and impulsive actions. At times, it can suggest being overly cautious and a need to be more playful and free-spirited.

Love and Relationships

The Fool can signal a relationship that is giddy with excitement and love. There is an air of carefree spontaneity and excitement. Those looking for relationships may find a new romance that is light and full of fun. Commitment may not be at the forefront when The Fool appears. Sometimes this card asks for optimism and a positive outlook in new relationships.

Career and Wealth

A new job or business opportunity may be in the works with The Fool in a career and wealth reading. There may be a positive shift occurring to reinvigorate a stagnant situation financially or at work. The Fool encourages new ventures and a fearless mindset to help one advance materially.

Success and Happiness

The Fool is a very happy, positive card with an energy of encouragement. This card can signify a good outcome or exciting news. Going with the flow and expecting a positive outcome can be part of the message. We are reminded to trust that things will work out.

Wild Card

The Fool can reveal a need to prepare for mishaps along the way or a deviation from the original path. Lack of planning and carefree attitudes may reveal weak organization or structure. Ultimately, we arrive at our destination, but it may be a tumultuous ride. Travel lightly and with ease.

THE MAGICIAN

THE MAGICIAN

NUMEROLOGY: **Potential**

ASTROLOGY: **Mercury**

ELEMENT: **Air**

COLORS: **Red, Yellow, Green, White**

SYMBOLS: **Infinity Symbol, Four Elements, Red Roses, Robe**

UPRIGHT KEY WORDS: Manifestation, Power, Magic, Taking Action, Mastered Skills

Upright Meaning

The Magician symbolizes already having everything you need to take inspired action within you. This is a card about manifesting your dreams and desires by using your inner power. The Magician may speak of specialized skills or knowledge and bringing your ideas into reality. We are also shown a spiritual element of aligning with one's higher purpose or consciousness.

REVERSED KEY WORDS: Latent Talent, Misalignment, Self-Doubt, Obstructed Creativity, Exploitation

Reversed Meaning

When The Magician is reversed, you are not living up to your full potential or using your gifts properly. There may be a creative block or feelings of weakness preventing a person from moving forward. A person may be pretending to be an expert at something they're not. The reversed Magician shows a need to realign and then act.

Love and Relationships

Usually a positive card, The Magician indicates happiness, devotion, and transitions toward deeper commitments. This card can also indicate a new phase or beginning in a relationship. For those who are unattached, The Magician encourages taking action and using creativity to attract new people into your life.

Career and Wealth

The Magician is portraying new opportunities and the chance to manifest what you seek. Career and wealth benefit from harnessing your skills and focusing on what you want. This card shows the potential to increase finances and advance in job positions using your talents and knowledge.

Success and Happiness

Manifestation plays a significant role with The Magician, and this card illustrates the importance of using your energy and knowledge to bring your dreams to fruition. When The Magician appears, great potential is possible. The Magician shows positive changes and transformation.

Wild Card

The Magician can refer to the need for spiritual connections and alignment with your higher consciousness. This card can present the opportunity to develop your spiritual or intuitive side and connect to yourself on a deeper level. We are reminded that we often have everything we need inside of us—we just have to put it all together.

THE HIGH PRIESTESS

THE HIGH PRIESTESS

NUMEROLOGY: **Duality**

ASTROLOGY: **Moon**

ELEMENT: **Water**

COLORS: **Blue, Yellow, White, Black, Red**

SYMBOLS: **Pomegranates, Cross, Moon, Pillar, Crown, Scroll**

Upright Meaning

The High Priestess is deeply connected to our intuition and inner knowing. This card encourages looking beyond the veil, balancing between the conscious and the subconscious. Hidden truths, divine feminine energy, and spiritual enlightenment are all aspects of The High Priestess. We are encouraged to tap into our intuition and be aware of hidden knowledge. The High Priestess asks us to connect to our feminine energy and balance it with our masculine energy.

REVERSED KEY WORDS: Disconnection, Disengagement, Secrecy, Repression

Reversed Meaning

The High Priestess reversed reveals that we have not been listening to our own intuition and instincts. You may be ignoring your inner voice or not expressing yourself. When reversed, this card can indicate a need for stillness and reflection. There may be a need to quiet your mind or meditate. Reversed, The High Priestess can also highlight self-doubt or a lack of faith.

Love and Relationships

In love and relationships, The High Priestess illustrates intimacy and honesty. There is a need for patience for those seeking partnership and those already committed. The High Priestess asks you to trust your intuition when it comes to your relationships. Additionally, this card acknowledges feminine and sexual energy in relationships.

Career and Wealth

Discretion is called for financially when The High Priestess is revealed in career and wealth readings. Share your financial details sparingly and with caution. In your career, there may be a mentor entering the scene to guide you. Use your intuition to navigate your career and finances.

Success and Happiness

The High Priestess shows an opportunity for success and happiness, but you must have faith in yourself and trust intuition. Pay attention to hidden influences and stay on your path without distraction. Release fear and listen to your inner wisdom.

Wild Card

Creative inspiration is abundant with The High Priestess, with the potential to flourish. This card can highlight a need to tap into feminine energy, regardless of your gender, and nurture yourself from a place of compassion and empathy. You are asked to embrace your intuition and inner wisdom and channel your energy creatively.

THE EMPRESS

THE EMPRESS

NUMEROLOGY: Creation

ASTROLOGY: Venus

ELEMENT: Earth

COLORS: Orange, Red, Yellow, Green, White

SYMBOLS: Crown, Stars, Robe, Pomegranates, Wheat, Scepter, Cushion

Upright Meaning

The Empress is a card of femininity, nurturing, and abundance. There is a motherly energy to the meaning, as well as the energy of fertility. The Empress signifies beauty and sensual and creative expression. Growth, gratitude, and prosperity are expressed. There is an emphasis on connecting to and appreciating nature with The Empress.

REVERSED KEY WORDS: Dependence, Obstructed Creativity, Stagnant, Materialistic

Reversed Meaning

The Empress reversed characterizes actions from a place of logic instead of the heart. A person may be feeling stuck or blocked, especially creatively. Reversed, there are possibilities of materialism and a lack of freedom. Self-care is encouraged, as well as a need to connect to nature and Mother Earth with The Empress reversed. Additionally, there may be an overbearing or codependent characteristic holding a person back.

Love and Relationships

Fertility, pregnancy, or marriage are possible with The Empress in love and relationships. The Empress shows nurturing partnerships full of support and commitment. Sensual elements within this card also suggest sexual chemistry. For those looking for relationships, encouraging prospects are on the way with The Empress.

Career and Wealth

Financially, prospects have the potential to flourish and prove abundant with The Empress. You may also be feeling generous and prone to sharing your wealth. Your career may be going through a more creative period, or you may be feeling more passionate about your work. Ideas and inspiration are thriving.

Success and Happiness

The Empress often denotes a positive outcome for success and happiness. This card encourages self-care and nurturing as a way to flourish. Self-love and acceptance are key to happiness with The Empress. Finding appreciation through nature and expressing gratitude are elements of this card for achieving success and growth.

Wild Card

Grounding in nature can be a significant message with The Empress. There is often a need to find the beauty of Mother Earth and connect on a more natural level. Allowing things to flow naturally and exploring spirituality are encouraged, along with following your intuition.

THE EMPEROR

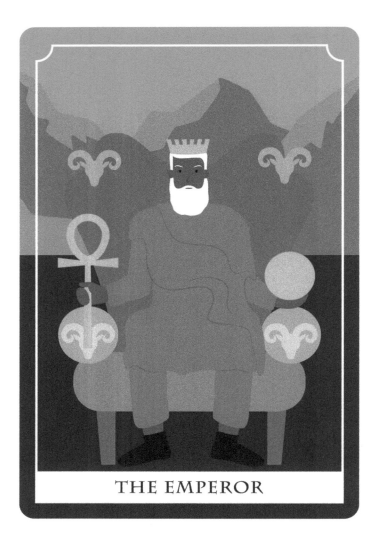

THE EMPEROR

NUMEROLOGY: **Stability**

ASTROLOGY: **Aries**

ELEMENT: **Fire**

COLORS: **Red, Yellow, Orange, Blue, White**

SYMBOLS: **Ankh, Crown, Robe, Orb, Ram's Head, Beard, Mountains**

UPRIGHT KEY WORDS: Foundation, Structure, Authority, Empowerment, Leadership

Upright Meaning

The Emperor embodies masculine energy and powerful leadership. This card speaks of stability, structure, and foundations being established. Rules and laws are adhered to, with The Emperor being worldly and intelligent. There is a paternal element, as well as fearlessness and discipline. The Emperor is in control, responsible, and prone to taking charge of situations.

REVERSED KEY WORDS: Rigid, Controlling, Immature, Abusive, Directionless

Reversed Meaning

There is a possibility of power being abused or misused when The Emperor is reversed. A person may be overly controlling and a tyrant, going from fatherly guidance to excessive belligerence. It can indicate immaturity and a lack of clear direction. Self-discipline may be needed, along with stepping up and taking charge. Reversed, The Emperor can portray delayed progress in endeavors.

Love and Relationships

Relationships may have a focus on logic and common sense as opposed to romance and playfulness. The Emperor can indicate a solid relationship and strong commitment but may lack emotional expression. Those seeking relationships are encouraged to be open and honest about their feelings when meeting new people.

Career and Wealth

Finances may need more control and responsibility. The Emperor suggests more fiscal discipline is needed to ensure increased revenue. Discipline and organization may be in order when The Emperor arrives regarding your career, as well. However, this card can also show career advancement and success from hard work and dedication.

Success and Happiness

The Emperor is a powerful card with an impact, embodying stability and structure. In readings, this card can portray a positive outcome if one stays diligent in planning. Success and happiness are possible through hard work. There are also elements of achievement and tangible results.

Wild Card

As the counterpart to The Empress, The Emperor signifies masculine energy. In readings, this card can indicate a need for balance between the two or encourage embracing masculine energy at this time. This card can also show a need for grounding and stabilizing yourself and being mindful to not push yourself too hard.

THE HIEROPHANT

NUMEROLOGY: Disruption

ASTROLOGY: Taurus

ELEMENT: Earth

COLORS: Red, Yellow, Blue, White

SYMBOLS: Cross, Crown, Pillar, Robe, Finger Sign, Keys

UPRIGHT KEY WORDS: Conformity, Tradition, Spiritual Knowledge, Religion, Institutions, Convention

Upright Meaning

The Hierophant (a priest who interprets sacred mysteries) relates to belief systems and religious structures and traditions. This card can refer to a leader, teacher, guide, or religious mentor, as well as the institutions associated with these people. There is often a sense of conformity and staying within rules and structures when this card appears. One may feel confined by authority or societal norms.

REVERSED KEY WORDS: Freedom, Breaking Free, Rebellion, Personal Thought

Reversed Meaning

Breaking free from the dictates of conventional norms and societal standards is illustrated when The Hierophant is reversed. A person may be acting rebelliously or thinking for themselves. Someone may be challenging the status quo and going within for their answers. They are encouraged to do things their own way and follow their own beliefs. Alternatively, a person may be misrepresenting themselves or passing along misinformation.

Love and Relationships

The Hierophant as a religious figure can indicate marriage in relationships. Partnerships with this card are often traditional, safe, and secure. Shared values and long-term commitments are likely. There may be approval and respect from peers and family. For those seeking love, The Hierophant is a positive sign for a new and stable relationship approaching.

Career and Wealth

This card suggests successful outcomes at work, particularly when collaborating with others. Follow protocol and play it safe with your career for the time being. There may be a boss or mentor who will work to help you advance and move forward. Financially, this card suggests low risk and traditional methods to manage your money.

Success and Happiness

The Hierophant speaks of fulfillment on your path, encouraging you to seek harmony and understanding of self. This card can be more neutral in meaning, yet it highlights growth and development through conventional wisdom. The Hierophant portrays the act of bringing things together.

Wild Card

This card can reveal a need to develop a community bond in a person's life, such as joining a club, group, educational institution, or team. This can also mean a spiritual group, such as meditation or yoga. The Hierophant suggests finding comfort among others with common values or goals.

THE LOVERS

THE LOVERS

NUMEROLOGY: **Harmony**

ASTROLOGY: **Venus**

ELEMENT: **Air**

COLORS: **Purple, Red, Green, Yellow, Blue**

SYMBOLS: **Angel, Apple, Snake, Tree, Flames, Clouds**

UPRIGHT KEY WORDS: Love, Relationships, Choices, Harmony, Union

Upright Meaning

The Lovers commonly refers to relationships that have a deep bond and connection. While this card usually refers to romantic bonds, it can also refer to special friendships and family connections. There are elements of balance, harmony, trust, and honesty when this card appears in readings. The Lovers also represents choices, unification, and personal values. This card speaks of deep love, spiritual unions, and ideal relationships.

REVERSED KEY WORDS: Disharmony, Misalignment, Conflict, Self-Love

Reversed Meaning

Conflicting values or mismatched beliefs are often portrayed when The Lovers is reversed. Relationships may need to be put on hold, or there may be a struggle to communicate effectively. This card can indicate that you are misaligned with your partner at the moment. Outside of relationships, you may be facing a difficult decision or struggling with inner turmoil. The need for self-love is often brought to attention when The Lovers is reversed.

Love and Relationships

Strong relationship commitments and special bonds are found with The Lovers. This card speaks of deep love and unity, and rekindled romance is likely. At times, this card can indicate a choice that may arise within a relationship. For those seeking companionship, The Lovers is a positive card, suggesting new love is on the way.

Career and Wealth

There is likely a serious choice to be made if The Lovers appears in career and wealth readings. This could refer to decisions with expenses or changes at work. Positive partnerships could be formed at work, and they even have the potential to turn romantic.

Success and Happiness

The Lovers is a positive card and represents an opening up of good times or happiness. This card explains that to obtain success and happiness, you must resolve internal conflicts and make carefully thought-out decisions.

Wild Card

Self-love and inner harmony are highlighted with The Lovers. It can show that you are encouraged to spend more time honoring, balancing, and loving yourself. This card reflects the act of staying true and authentic to yourself, aligning with your values, and being genuine in your approach.

THE CHARIOT

THE CHARIOT

NUMEROLOGY: Wisdom

ASTROLOGY: Moon

ELEMENT: Water

COLORS: Black, White, Blue, Yellow, Red

SYMBOLS: Moons, Crown, Stars, Armor, Sphinx, River

Upright Meaning

The Chariot symbolizes progress and setting things in motion. This is a very victorious and successful card, showcasing strong willpower and determination to move forward. Obstacles are overcome when The Chariot emerges, and it brings an air of wisdom. This card asks you to keep going and not be deterred as you stay the course. There are times when The Chariot represents literal movement or travel.

REVERSED KEY WORDS: Directionless, Weakness, Delays, Uncontrollable, Disorderly

Reversed Meaning

There is a lack of control when it comes to following your path. You could be overwhelmed and pulled in different directions. Plans may be delayed when The Chariot is reversed. Lack of willpower is portrayed by the reversal, along with a need to bring back your focus. If you are feeing powerless, the reversed Chariot encourages discipline and determination to get back on track.

Love and Relationships

Action may be needed in relationships when The Chariot rolls in, which means taking control of situations that may be affecting the stability of your partnership. The Chariot asks you to overcome issues causing disharmony. Those seeking love are encouraged to keep moving forward from past relationship hurts to make way for new companionship.

Career and Wealth

There is a lot of ambition and determination with The Chariot when it comes to your career. This card is a positive sign to move forward on ideas about your career, indicating things will align in your favor. Those looking for work are reassured with The Chariot. Financial obstacles are likely to be overcome with this card.

Success and Happiness

The Chariot shows you coming out the other side of a challenging situation in triumph. There is an element of increased motivation and self-control to persevere. This is a card of accomplishment and completion, leading to success and happiness. With The Chariot, expect hard work and willpower to pay off.

Wild Card

Spiritual journeys and actual physical travel are aspects of The Chariot. Chances are good that you are moving forward on your path in life or that you are about to visit someplace. You could be moving to a new location or spending time away for a while.

STRENGTH

STRENGTH

NUMEROLOGY: **Accomplishment**

ASTROLOGY: **Sun**

ELEMENT: **Fire**

COLORS: **Red, Yellow, White, Green, Blue**

SYMBOLS: **Lion, White Robe, Crown, Infinity Symbol, Greenery**

UPRIGHT KEY WORDS: Strength, Compassion, Courage, Transformation, Assertiveness, Grace

Upright Meaning

Strength represents inner strength and tenacity. This card portrays stamina, personal power, and the ability to fight through the fear. You are shown the need to calm the chaos around you with your grace and influence. Strength portrays having the ability to control your instincts when you're feeling emotional or raw, turning the rage and anger into a more balanced or compassionate response.

REVERSED KEY WORDS: Weakness, Limitations, Self-Doubt, Emotional

Reversed Meaning

Disempowerment or feeling a lack of confidence is an attribute of Strength reversed. You may be feeling vulnerable, with low energy or a lack of belief in yourself. Temporary challenges ahead are possible with this card. Additionally, Strength reversed shows the possibility of an out-of-control temper or lashing out. There could be aggressive elements at play.

Love and Relationships

Loving relationships based on care and compassion are embodied by the Strength card. Passionate romance is likely to be found. There is a risk that the relationship may have emotional outbursts or fiery disagreements. Those seeking love are encouraged to act with confidence to draw in their ideal partner.

Career and Wealth

Leaps and strides are possible with Strength, provided you rein in any uncontrollable instincts or outbursts. Find ways to channel your drive and passion so that you can work in harmony toward bigger goals. Finances will be in a good place if you act responsibly without impulsive spending.

Success and Happiness

Better times are on the horizon when the Strength card turns up, and this card encourages you to know that things will get better, so have endurance and perseverance. Direct your energy into practices that bring you more harmony so you can align with a joyful and prosperous future.

Wild Card

There are times when the Strength card can indicate a person in recovery from addiction, particularly drugs or alcohol. This card shows overcoming adversity and taming inner turmoil with grace and strength. Patience and deliberate action toward wellness and harmony are found with the Strength card.

THE HERMIT

THE HERMIT

NUMEROLOGY: **Fulfillment**

ASTROLOGY: **Virgo**

ELEMENT: **Earth**

COLORS: **Yellow, White, Blue, Gray**

SYMBOLS: **Mountaintop, Lantern, Staff, Beard**

UPRIGHT KEY WORDS: Going Within, Introspective, Soul Searching, Alone, Wisdom

Upright Meaning

The Hermit characterizes self-exploration and going within to do some soul searching. This card asks you to take a break from the noise and distraction to be introspective. Take time alone and allow your inner wisdom to guide you on this part of your journey. The Hermit offers answers to the questions you seek through this period of deep contemplation.

REVERSED KEY WORDS: Exile, Withdrawal, Isolated

Reversed Meaning

There are two different meanings to The Hermit reversed. On one hand, you may need to go much deeper into your personal reflection and take time away from the crowd. On the other, you may have taken it to an extreme and isolated yourself from loved ones and society. When this card is reversed, you may find yourself as an actual hermit, having shut out everyone around you. It is now time to reconnect with people.

Love and Relationships

When The Hermit emerges, a relationship may be at a point where it requires a break for introspection and much-needed time alone. Both partners are advised to do some soul searching to better understand themselves and what they need. Those seeking a relationship may be about to meet someone and end a period of loneliness when The Hermit shows up in readings.

Career and Wealth

Purpose may be lacking in your career, or you feel as though you are not on the right path with your work. The Hermit reveals a need for you to figure out what would make you feel fulfilled in your career. Financially, you may be focused on material spending and could benefit from investing and saving at this time.

Success and Happiness

The Hermit speaks of discernment and wisdom, and to attain success and happiness you are encouraged to be deliberate in your thoughts and actions. Take time to think before taking the next step. Seek meaning, depth, and purpose on your journey to achieve happiness.

Wild Card

The Hermit is a deeply personal card and can reveal a need for spiritual healing and reflection. It may suggest shifting your beliefs and reforming your personal principles and ideals. The Hermit advises you to follow your own path of independent thinking and ways of being.

WHEEL OF FORTUNE

WHEEL OF FORTUNE

NUMEROLOGY: Completion

ASTROLOGY: Jupiter

ELEMENT: Fire

COLORS: Red, Yellow, Orange, White, Blue

SYMBOLS: Symbolic Letters, Four Elements, Snake, Anubis, Sphinx, Torah

UPRIGHT KEY WORDS: Good Fortune, Karma, Cycles, Luck, Serendipity, Fate, Positive Change

Upright Meaning

Wheel of Fortune embodies the turning of a cycle, usually for the better. Good luck is arriving, and there is often a message of destiny or a happy change of events. This card shows you that things can go either way with the turn of the wheel. The saying "what goes up must come down" is associated with this card, and what you put out you receive back.

REVERSED KEY WORDS: Misfortune, Resistance, Disruption, Setbacks, Downturn, Unexpected Change

Reversed Meaning

Expect a reversal of luck or good fortune. There is unexpected change that relates to setbacks or misfortune, but you are given the opportunity to shift things in your favor and know that a down cycle is temporary. The Wheel reversed can shed light on your resistance to change and asks you to become more open to going with the flow and surrendering the need for control.

Love and Relationships

Unexpected changes arise when Wheel of Fortune appears in love readings. These upheavals are temporary, and this card advises you to navigate the turns together. These changes can be positive or negative. For those seeking a relationship, things are turning in your favor for a new love interest to appear.

Career and Wealth

Big changes are coming in your career, and the wheel is turning. This often speaks in your favor; however, the Wheel may reflect an approaching challenge at work. Be careful with your spending if you are doing well financially. Those struggling may see a positive change of luck.

Success and Happiness

Wheel of Fortune indicates happy changes ahead, with good luck and a shift in the right direction. You may find situations start falling into alignment, as this is usually a "yes" card that shows success and happiness are on the way.

Wild Card

This can be a time when you need to break a cycle in your life, behaviors, or thought patterns. You may be caught up in a repeating cycle, and the only way to shift into a better place is by making a big change to move forward. The Wheel encourages you to break negative cycles and become more aligned.

JUSTICE

JUSTICE

NUMEROLOGY: Balance

ASTROLOGY: Libra

ELEMENT: Air

COLORS: Red, Yellow, Green, Purple, Gray

SYMBOLS: Pillar, Sword, Scale, Crown, Robe, Shoe

UPRIGHT KEY WORDS: Justice, Truth, Fair, Honesty, Just Outcomes, Legal Business

Upright Meaning

Justice calls for balance in your life and the ability to hold yourself accountable for your actions. Despite it being a card of truth, law, and fairness, there is also a compassionate element to Justice. This card asks you to seek truth with discernment and to weigh matters carefully before making major decisions. You are accountable for the consequences of your choices.

REVERSED KEY WORDS: Unfairly Judged, Dishonest, No Accountability, Unjust

Reversed Meaning

When this card is reversed, it may imply that you acted with dishonesty and must atone for your transgressions. You are being asked to be honest with yourself and acknowledge your mistakes. On the other hand, you may be criticizing yourself unfairly and giving harsh self-judgement. Reversed, Justice can also find you in a situation where you are being unfairly judged or facing injustice.

Love and Relationships

Fairness in relationships, along with compromise, are highlighted by the Justice card. The way you treat your partner will reflect back to you in your relationship. Your actions serve as a mirror, so you are asked to love with honesty and fairness. Justice brings new and supportive romance to those seeking a relationship.

Career and Wealth

Integrity remains at the forefront at work when the Justice card appears. Stay truthful and fair, knowing that this course of action will likely lead to a favorable turn in your career. Additionally, a work situation may resolve in your favor. Financially, expect stability.

Success and Happiness

Justice indicates balance and fairness, so if this card appears when success and happiness are in question, this can be a positive sign. This card seeks the best solution in a situation, resolving outstanding issues for a just and fair outcome. Justice acts with integrity and will reward those who act accordingly.

Wild Card

Legal cases or government institutions come into play with the Justice card. Those seeking fairness in a legal trial or a dispute are likely to see a fair and just outcome in their favor. Wrongs are made right and all of the facts are carefully examined when the Justice card emerges.

THE HANGED MAN

THE HANGED MAN

NUMEROLOGY: Growth

ASTROLOGY: Neptune

ELEMENT: Water

COLORS: Blue, Red, Yellow, Brown, Green

SYMBOLS: Halo, Cross, Rope, Red Pants, Triangle

Upright Meaning

New perspectives are in order with The Hanged Man. Shift your way of thinking to overcome a situation or open the door for new opportunities. You may be encouraged to pause or take a break before proceeding, or to really contemplate and think things through. Surrender and see things in a new light. Step back and allow things to unfold, and process your thoughts before acting.

REVERSED KEY WORDS: Resistance, Undecided, Status Quo, Obstruction

Reversed Meaning

Rest is necessary but being ignored when The Hanged Man is in the reversed position. Here, you are filling your time with tasks to distract yourself from your thoughts. This card is asking you to pause and reflect before continuing—and you may be ignoring this advice. You may be feeling blocked by situations in your life and fighting the need to surrender to allow things to unfold. If you have been stalling taking action on something, now is the time to make your move.

Love and Relationships

Those seeking romance are advised not to rush or force things before the time is right with The Hanged Man. Couples are asked to sacrifice or compromise for the benefit of the relationship. Fresh perspectives or reassessment may be needed before continuing further. Shake things up if you are both in a rut.

Career and Wealth

Timing is everything with work right now, and there may be factors beyond your control. The Hanged Man suggests that waiting or taking a pause is necessary before moving to your next career phase. Take this time to consider what it is you really want. Financially, you are advised to think outside of the box and find new ways to invest or grow your profits.

Success and Happiness

The Hanged Man helps direct you toward success and happiness by encouraging you to think things through before acting on impulse, allowing more grounded and well-thought-out choices. Reflection and patience can pay off when you are ready to move forward.

Wild Card

This card can highlight an area of your life that may be stagnant, prompting you to consider what it is you may need to release for healing and growth. There are times The Hanged Man asks you to have faith and reassess what is not actually working for you.

DEATH

DEATH

NUMEROLOGY: Structure

ASTROLOGY: Scorpio

ELEMENT: Water

COLORS: Black, White, Blue, Yellow, Green

SYMBOLS: Skeleton, Black Armor, White Horse, Black Flag, White Rose, Boat, Sunset

Upright Meaning

Death speaks of significant transformation and transitions. Think "out with the old, in with the new." When Death emerges it signals a period of rebirth and change. Something must end so new doors can open. A major shift is occurring and may be unexpected. This card speaks of letting go and accepting inevitable change.

REVERSED KEY WORDS: Resisting Change, Rigidness, Stagnation

Reversed Meaning

Resistance to change and reluctance to move forward are portrayed by Death reversed. This creates a feeling of stagnation or being stuck. You are encouraged to surrender and allow transformation to occur. Death reversed asks you to be mindful that you are not repeating negative behaviors or patterns.

Love and Relationships

Your relationship is about to take a new direction, presenting a change in the dynamic of your interactions. At times, this card could indicate the end of a relationship. The Death card in a love reading is not necessarily negative, however, as the shift could be exciting, such as an engagement. Those looking for love are encouraged to release thoughts and behaviors that may be holding them back from partnership.

Career and Wealth

Career changes you have been considering are recommended when the Death card shows up. Work may be experiencing shifts and adjustments that you should not try to resist. New doors could open. Financial loss is possible, or a change in your budget.

Success and Happiness

This card reveals that change is not always for the worse and embracing new ways can be beneficial. Death highlights the need to transform so that you can better align with what brings you harmony and joy. Take this card as a sign that things are about to change, or that you need to make changes to ensure long-term success and happiness.

Wild Card

There are times when the Death card represents the death of your ego. The card can express a deeply personal transformation in which you are privately enduring many changes that shape the way you think and that help you adjust your views and beliefs. You are moving forward into a new version of yourself, experiencing a rebirth.

TEMPERANCE

TEMPERANCE

NUMEROLOGY: Change

ASTROLOGY: Sagittarius

ELEMENT: Fire

COLORS: White, Blue, Yellow, Red, Green

SYMBOLS: Angel Wings, Robe, Triangle, Water, Cup, Path, Mountains, Crown

Upright Meaning

Temperance asks for tolerance, patience, and balance. The "middle road." This card speaks of blending highs and lows as you navigate situations. It can also mean combining elements creatively or in relationships. Temperance portrays calm and moderation, advising calm and calling you to pause before reacting to situations.

REVERSED KEY WORDS: Imbalance, Impatient, Excessive, Unreasonable

Reversed Meaning

You have been taking measures and behaviors to an extreme with excessive actions and indulgence. Temperance reversed implies you have lost control and are acting unreasonably instead of with grace and moderation. This card also speaks of an imbalance in your life that needs attention. Your priorities may not align with your desired direction, so Temperance encourages you to reassess.

Love and Relationships

Patience and understanding are needed in your relationship. Temperance is showing you the need for compromise to achieve balance and harmony in your relationship. If you are looking for love, Temperance suggests patience until the time is right.

Career and Wealth

Dedication and a calm approach are needed at work when Temperance appears. Your career path will benefit from devotion and staying balanced between life and work. Financially, you are inspired to build your savings while you balance splurging and enjoying life.

Success and Happiness

Temperance signifies the act of slow and steady progress leading to positive results. To achieve success and happiness, this card suggests moderation, balance, and patience, along with staying the course. Mixing different elements creatively as needed will help you achieve your goals sooner, allowing you to go with the flow.

Wild Card

Temperance can sometimes reveal confidence and staying empowered during times of adversity. This card promotes higher learning and inner growth, allowing you to expand your awareness and the way you approach situations. There is a spiritual element with Temperance, prompting you to connect to your higher self.

THE DEVIL

NUMEROLOGY: **Union**

ASTROLOGY: **Capricorn**

ELEMENT: **Earth**

COLORS: **Black, Red, Gray, White, Green**

SYMBOLS: **Chains, Bat Wings, Inverted Pentagram, Torch, Vulcan Salute, Horns, Tail, Grapes**

UPRIGHT KEY WORDS: Attachment, Addiction, Dependence, Shadow Self, Sexuality, Illusion, Oppression

Upright Meaning

The Devil reveals our shadow selves and our negative attributes like addictions, attachments, and dependencies. We are shown that lack of control is only an illusion and breaking free is still an option. Your constraints are actually quite loose, and you are not as dependent on other people or circumstances as you may think.

REVERSED KEY WORDS: Detachment, Release, Self-Exploration, Liberation, Discernment, Responsible

Reversed Meaning

Reversed, The Devil characterizes the intentional release of attachments and what no longer serves you. You are on the brink of transformation but must first purge bad habits. Use your discernment to liberate yourself from what keeps you trapped.

Love and Relationships

Sexuality and lust are at the forefront when The Devil appears in love and relationship readings. There is an element of temptation and the possibility of selfishness when it comes to gratification. This card can also reveal a codependent or unhealthy relationship. More mildly, it portrays having fun together.

Career and Wealth

You are feeling dependent on your job or stuck in your career with The Devil. You feel you have no options or are trapped by the circumstances. Release yourself from that mentality so you can move forward. Mind your finances when it comes to gambling or risky behavior with money.

Success and Happiness

The Devil can signal decadence or appealing situations that lead to success and happiness. This brings a risk of becoming materialistic or too attached to what brings you happiness. The Devil reminds you to remain aware of your behavior so as not to go overboard or get out of control.

Wild Card

The Devil can represent a strong bond or attachment between two people. While this often indicates a connection between two lovers, it can also be between family members. When closely connected relationships are shown with The Devil, you are cautioned to use your guidance and set boundaries so as not to become overly attached or dependent.

THE TOWER

THE TOWER

NUMEROLOGY: **Understanding**

ASTROLOGY: **Mars**

ELEMENT: **Fire**

COLORS: **Yellow, Red, Blue, Black, Gray**

SYMBOLS: **Crown, Fire, Clouds, Mountain, Lightning, 22 Flames**

Upright Meaning

The Tower is a card of chaos and extreme disruption. Prepare for sudden and unexpected upheaval and the crumbling of a foundation in your life. Something is torn down to be rebuilt in a new and improved way. The Tower represents moments of clarity and revelation, often with a shocking or destructive truth being revealed. This card brings about change that paves the way for new beginnings and evolution.

REVERSED KEY WORDS: Aftereffects, Crisis Averted, Resistance, Inner Change

Reversed Meaning

Reversed, The Tower shows a resistance to change and fighting the inevitable. You may be avoiding surrender to the circumstances around you, prolonging your pain or turmoil. This card may also depict your state after a life-changing event. At times, upheaval has been avoided when The Tower is reversed. The Tower reversed also reflects inner change on a deeply personal level that leads to transformation.

Love and Relationships

Relationships may be suffering from instability at the moment or on the verge of collapsing. There is also the possibility of a major change or revelation within the relationship that shifts the status quo. If you are looking for love, this card encourages inner reflection and a shifting of perspective before entering new relationships.

Career and Wealth

External elements could be causing disruption at work, leaving chaos and uncertainty. The Tower highlights the stress that upheaval might place on your career. Difficult times are temporary and remove obstacles for future endeavors. Emergency funds are suggested in case of sudden expenses or the loss of a job.

Success and Happiness

There can be exhilarating situations with The Tower that reflect success and happiness. When this card appears before massive change, we are reminded that what comes after can be beautiful and a positive new start.

Wild Card

The Tower can represent a spiritual awakening in which our beliefs and thoughts are shaken up and torn down to make way for change. This card reveals the emotional turmoil that comes with that spiritual awakening, along with the hope and comfort of divine guidance and serenity afterward.

THE STAR

THE STAR

NUMEROLOGY: **Attainment**

ASTROLOGY: **Aquarius**

ELEMENT: **Air**

COLORS: **Blue, Yellow, White, Green, Red**

SYMBOLS: **Stars, Water, Bird, Mountain**

Upright Meaning

Peace and calm prevail after a period of turmoil, and The Star reflects this newfound serenity. Faith is restored and hope is renewed. This card is a positive reminder of all that is possible. Divine connections come with The Star, along with healing and feelings of purpose. Magic is rekindled and you feel elated. The Star lifts your spirits and prompts you to keep going with your newly inspired optimism.

REVERSED KEY WORDS: Disappointment, Delays, Pessimism, Doubt, Disconnect

Reversed Meaning

When The Star emerges reversed, chances are you have lost your faith and are feeling hopeless. You are feeling doubtful about yourself and your future or are experiencing disappointment. There may be delays in your circumstances that leave you pessimistic. Disconnection from self or spirit has you seeking inspiration and purpose. The Star beckons you to rise above this test of endurance and overcome the challenge.

Love and Relationships

The Star offers hope in relationships. If you are seeking love and partnership, The Star indicates a hopeful and positive outcome. New love is likely, and keeping your optimism high contributes to manifesting a new relationship. Those currently involved can see some healing in their relationship, allowing more unity.

Career and Wealth

Have faith in achieving your career goals, as The Star appears with a message of positivity for new opportunities with work. New positions, career shifts, or promotions are likely. Calm periods are also approaching if work has been hectic. Finances may be headed in a good direction.

Success and Happiness

This card often serves as a positive indicator of good things to come and is meant to inspire. The Star offers hope and excitement in readings when it comes to success and joy. Self-care and reinvigorating your spirits are sometimes reflected in The Star as a path toward happiness.

Wild Card

Generosity is an element of The Star that can appear at times. You are likely someone who gives freely and without expecting a return. You believe in paying it forward and share your blessings with others so they, too, may grow and transform into the best versions of themselves.

THE MOON

NUMEROLOGY: **Fulfillment**

ASTROLOGY: **Pisces**

ELEMENT: **Water**

COLORS: **Yellow, Blue, Green, Gray, Red**

SYMBOLS: **Dog, Wolf, Moon, Towers, Water Pool, Crayfish**

UPRIGHT KEY WORDS: Intuition, Mystery, Instinct, Illusion, Subconscious, Anxiety

Upright Meaning

Through illusion and mystery The Moon speaks of your intuition and discerning the truth in matters. Nothing is really as it seems. Your subconscious thoughts are coming to the surface to be confronted. Anxiety may be running high, and old wounds need attention or healing. The emergence of The Moon indicates a need to trust your instincts and look further. Uncertainty can be conquered by going within.

REVERSED KEY WORDS: Clarity, Illumination, Waning, Confusion, Emotional Restraint

Reversed Meaning

The anxieties and emotional turmoil from the subconscious that appear with The Moon are starting to subside when the card is reversed. You are finding relief and liberation from the worries and troubles that surfaced. You may be holding yourself back emotionally and not allowing yourself to fully step into your light.

Love and Relationships

Misunderstandings and illusions occur in relationships with The Moon. Confusion or uncertainty can be causing complications. Insecurity is arising from miscommunication. It signals caution when entering new relationships, as all may not be as it appears. Watch for deception.

Career and Wealth

Lack of clarity with your work is causing some confusion and leaving you feeling unsettled. Your career can benefit from uncovering more information about situations so you can make informed decisions. The Moon in financial readings suggests waiting on major money moves until you have more information.

Success and Happiness

Follow your instinct when it comes to your fulfilling your dreams. To achieve your goals you must have full awareness of the situation. Do not let your anxieties or past issues distract you from your path. Release your worries and allow your instincts to help guide you to happiness.

Wild Card

The Moon card can place special emphasis on your intuition in relation to the cycles of the moon. You are guided to create a ritual for yourself to connect to your intuition and work on manifesting your dreams and goals. The Moon aids in creating intentions for yourself and also embraces divine feminine energy.

THE SUN

NUMEROLOGY: Completion

ASTROLOGY: Sun

ELEMENT: Fire

COLORS: Yellow, Red, White, Blue

SYMBOLS: Sun, Sunflowers, Child, White Horse

UPRIGHT KEY WORDS: Joy, Positivity, Happiness, Success, Brightness, Freedom, Fulfillment

Upright Meaning

This is a very positive and encouraging card to receive in readings. The Sun represents joy, happiness, success, and positivity. Good news is on the way, and better times are ahead. The Sun shows you that your warmth and brightness carry you through the hard times and draw others to you. This card signifies confidence and empowerment. You are experiencing liberation and feeling fulfilled.

REVERSED KEY WORDS: Happiness Postponed, Inner Child, Excessive Hope, Deferred Success

Reversed Meaning

The Sun reversed usually depicts the same meaning as the card upright but to a lesser extent. Obstacles are temporary with The Sun reversed, and good news is still arriving—it's just delayed or hindered. You are prompted to connect to your inner child and play and to be joyful and free. Reversed, The Sun indicates you may need a boost of optimism to keep going. Alternatively, at times this position shows that you are overly hopeful to the point of being unrealistic.

Love and Relationships

Your positive outlook and radiant energy will help draw in romance and new partnership. The Sun asks you to shine your light, allowing others to gravitate to you. Relationships are full of happiness, harmony, and warmth with The Sun. Celebrations and blessings are likely, leading to more feelings of fulfillment.

Career and Wealth

New career opportunities are possible with The Sun. You are about to receive promotions or career changes for the better. The Sun portrays a satisfying and happy work environment. Finances are in a good position, and light will shine on any areas that need attention.

Success and Happiness

Success and clarity for the future are portrayed by The Sun. This card exhibits peace and calm, along with being uplifted. The Sun exemplifies celebrations and sunny breakthroughs. Both short-term and long-term happiness can be expected to emerge, and staying positive is encouraged to draw in success when The Sun appears.

Wild Card

The Sun can represent physical energy and good health. This card reveals that you are about to experience an energy boost. You are invigorated and revitalized with The Sun. This signifies you are feeling very positive and optimistic, bursting with abundance and radiant energy.

JUDGEMENT

JUDGEMENT

NUMEROLOGY: Choices

ASTROLOGY: Pluto

ELEMENT: Fire

COLORS: Red, Blue, Yellow, White, Gray

SYMBOLS: Archangel Gabriel, Trumpet, Graves, Mountains, Cross

UPRIGHT KEY WORDS: Rebirth, Judgement, Awakening, Raising Consciousness, Life Purpose, Renewal

Upright Meaning

Judgement appears when you are at a crossroads or about to make a significant decision. This card is about rebirth and renewal and indicates you are near the end of a situation. Rise up now and connect to your inner calling or life purpose. You are awakening and raising your level of consciousness.

REVERSED KEY WORDS: Doubt, Fear, Mistrust, Holding Back, Unwanted Change, Ignoring Purpose

Reversed Meaning

Reversed, Judgement reveals that you are ignoring the messages being sent to you because they make you uncomfortable. Your purpose or new opportunities are being dismissed due to self-doubt or fear, thus preventing you from moving into a better place or transforming into a better version of yourself. Freedom comes when you accept and love yourself.

Love and Relationships

Love is renewed with the Judgement card. Relationships need some adjustment to clear the way for positive change, and communication enables this to occur. Issues are being brought to light so you and your partner can work through them. If you are seeking a relationship, Judgement encourages you to learn from past love lessons to create new foundations going forward.

Career and Wealth

You are being called to follow your passion and awaken to work that fulfills you. Judgement shows that evaluating your actions at work is needed. Money matters improve through reflection on your financial habits.

Success and Happiness

Judgement brings you to a period of wholeness and restoration. Success and happiness are attainable now, and your new state of awareness will guide you toward feeling content. This card shows you are falling into alignment with a greater state of being and approaching a turning point.

Wild Card

When the Judgement card appears during times of struggle or challenge, it suggests that sharing your experience with others will offer much-needed support. This card points out that connecting with people who are going through similar trials will help you navigate your challenges with a sense of camaraderie and guidance.

THE WORLD

NUMEROLOGY: Growth

ASTROLOGY: Saturn

ELEMENT: Earth

COLORS: Blue, Green, Red, Yellow, Purple

SYMBOLS: Wreath, Magic Wand, Lion, Bull, Cherub, Eagle

UPRIGHT KEY WORDS: Completion, Accomplishment, Attainment, Full Circle, Success, Wholeness

Upright Meaning

The World arrives at the completion of a cycle, when you have attained fulfillment. "Having the world" is the phrase related to this card, portraying success and accomplishment. You are feeling whole and have come full circle with yourself or a situation. Endings are accomplished, and you will be celebrating your achievements. If you have yet to reach your conclusion, you are almost there.

REVERSED KEY WORDS: Delays, Stagnant, Closure, Bypass

Reversed Meaning

Success and completion are delayed when The World is reversed. Do not give up before reaching the finish line. You may be reaching a period of closure on a more personal level with The World in reverse. Inner work needs to be done to release the past and move forward.

Love and Relationships

Relationships are fulfilling and happy, and a new cycle may be approaching. You may be moving your union to the next level, such as marriage. There is gratitude and appreciation in relationships. If you are seeking love, this card invites you to feel whole with yourself first.

Career and Wealth

Celebrations are at hand in connection with your career or job position. Perhaps you have completed a project, received a promotion, or found your dream job. Your career gives you emotional satisfaction at this time, and you feel secure. Financial goals are being met, and splurges are possible.

Success and Happiness

The World promotes success and happiness, having completed your journey and reaching your destination. Situations are looking up, and things are falling into place. Perseverance brings harmony and balance to your life, and The World recognizes your achievements. You have reached a place of integration and joy.

Wild Card

There are times when The World represents travel and possibly foreign or long-term plans. In this case, The World is showing you appreciation for other people and their cultures. Awareness of the whole world is highlighted, with a newfound sense of global understanding.

CHAPTER 7

THE MINOR ARCANA: CUPS

THE SUITS OF THE MINOR ARCANA cards depict archetypes that reveal the current influences in our life and the interactions we encounter. These cards explore the people, surroundings, thoughts, and feelings associated with situations. Specifically, the Cups suit reflects our emotions, feelings, and intuition. Creativity and matters of the heart are also highlighted with Cups, along with romance and fantasy. Cups symbolically relate to the element of water. This chapter explains the key words and meanings for each card in the suit, from the Ace (which is one) through the King of Cups.

ACE OF CUPS

ACE OF CUPS

NUMEROLOGY: **Opportunity**

ASTROLOGY: **Pisces**

ELEMENT: **Water**

COLORS: **Blue, Yellow, Green, Gray**

SYMBOLS: **Dove, Chalice, Water, Streams, Cloud, Lotus Blossoms, Cross**

UPRIGHT KEY WORDS: Compassion, Love, New Partnerships, Grace, Creativity, Spirituality, Gift

Upright Meaning

Love flows through you with the Ace of Cups. Compassion and spiritual awareness are abundant, and you are full of love that radiates into the world. Creative opportunities are being presented, and creative expression is encouraged. You feel connected to others and are generous with your love and energy. New love or relationships of different kinds are possible. Unconditional love is an attribute of this card.

REVERSED KEY WORDS: Self-Love, Unrequited Love, Self-Care, Blocked Happiness

Reversed Meaning

Loving yourself is a theme with the Ace of Cups reversed. Your flow of love may be stunted, so work on self-care before trying to share your love. This card suggests you are repressing your emotions or not feeling the love you put out being returned. Your lack of emotional expression may result in hindered happiness until you release your inner emotions.

Love and Relationships

New relationships are beginning, and single people can look forward to romance approaching. Current relationships may shift to the next level, or the intimacy may deepen. Emotional growth is unfolding, and compassion is present. Use your intuition and go with the flow in love.

Career and Wealth

New projects are being pushed forward through a spark of inspiration, and your creativity is being explored. Work relationships are harmonious, and the Ace of Cups shows new opportunities and job offers. Take on new responsibilities with confidence at work. Financial help is on the way, and creative means can help earn more income.

Success and Happiness

Good things are coming your way with the Ace of Cups. It projects success, happiness, and positive outcomes. You are encouraged to stay open to new beginnings. This card shows a harmonic alignment unfolding, bringing love and compassion.

Wild Card

Fertility can be associated with the Ace of Cups. Birth or pregnancy may be imminent. At times, this card means symbolic birth, such as inspiration or ideas being sparked. These are projects you will invest a lot of time, love, and energy in. The Ace of Cups signifies conception in all its forms.

TWO OF CUPS

2 OF CUPS

NUMEROLOGY: **Balance**

ASTROLOGY: **Cancer**

ELEMENT: **Water**

COLORS: **Red, Yellow, Green, Blue, Brown**

SYMBOLS: **Caduceus, Lion's Head, Cup**

Upright Meaning

Love is flowing between you and another person with the Two of Cups. There is a deep connection, compassion, and understanding. You have a strong union and a harmonic relationship. This relationship may be in the early stages. This card highlights mutual attraction and connection. There is a mutually beneficial commitment between you and your partner.

REVERSED KEY WORDS: Uncommitted, Blocked Love, Parting, Disharmony, Self-Love

Reversed Meaning

Self-love and going within to learn how to love yourself unconditionally are apparent with the Two of Cups reversed. It shows your need for self-acceptance and the ability to respect who you are. This card also reflects an imbalance or disharmony between you and your partner or with yourself. Relationships may be dissolving, or love may be conditional. Reversed, this card indicates a blockage or lack of flow in love.

Love and Relationships

New relationships based on unity are formed, full of harmony and balance. The Two of Cups signifies communication and support from your partner. Cooperation exists, and each person is growing as an individual while contributing to the relationship. Single people may meet a new partner with passionate and mutual attraction.

Career and Wealth

Relationships at work are very strong and positive right now. You are working well with others and may embark on a new career partnership with someone. Abundance is possible with the Two of Cups and your career. Financial matters are secure and stable, with fiscal balance.

Success and Happiness

Expect balance and harmony in your life with the Two of Cups. Positive energy is being sent your way, with outcomes looking favorable. This card speaks of unity and coming together, leading to success and happiness. You are invited to embrace life fully and with an open heart, encountering stability and abundance.

Wild Card

The Two of Cups can represent a business partnership that is built on a shared vision. You and your business partner are able to work on creations together because you are in sync and each offers something the other does not. Together, you work in harmony and have respect for each other, likely resulting in success.

THREE OF CUPS

3 OF CUPS

NUMEROLOGY: **Creation**

ASTROLOGY: **Cancer**

ELEMENT: **Water**

COLORS: **Red, Yellow, Blue, Green, Gray**

SYMBOLS: **Chalice, Robe, Flowers**

Upright Meaning

Celebration is abundant with the Three of Cups. This card finds you rejoicing with friends or family and often indicates strong female relationships. Close friendships are honored, and fun times are here. There is much laughter with the Three of Cups. A very social element presents itself, and you are encouraged to connect with other like-minded people to unwind and be joyful.

REVERSED KEY WORDS: Excess, Cancellation, Strained Friendships, Delayed Celebration, Independence

Reversed Meaning

Time alone to decompress and reevaluate friendships is needed with the Three of Cups reversed. You feel like you are alone or no longer fitting in with your circle of friends. This card asks you to go within to better understand what you would like to experience socially. At times, the Three of Cups reversed reveals overindulgence and excessive celebrating to the point of destruction.

Love and Relationships

People looking for relationships may find love and romance within their social circle. Friendships can turn into romance. Relationships may become cause for celebration and happy times ahead. Weddings, proposals, and other joyful occasions are likely.

Career and Wealth

Financially, you are in a position to celebrate, and you may be feeling generous as a result. Your career may find you attending various social events and work gatherings. Work relationships and collaborations are going well, and the overall environment is positive with the Three of Cups.

Success and Happiness

Moderation is important for success and happiness, as the Three of Cups signifies the possibility of overindulgence. This card invites you to find a balance with your celebrations to ensure long-term happiness. Overall, winning and victory are portrayed, with a positive outlook going forward.

Wild Card

Creative collaborations are indicated with the Three of Cups. Ideas and projects can really take off when you get this card, as it suggests working with others to create your vision. You are encouraged to explore your passions and expand your reach to others so they can experience your creations.

FOUR OF CUPS

4 OF CUPS

NUMEROLOGY: Planning

ASTROLOGY: Cancer

ELEMENT: Water

COLORS: Blue, Yellow, Green, Gray, Red

SYMBOLS: Tree, Chalice, Hill, Arm, Cloud

Upright Meaning

The Four of Cups portrays a need to turn down new opportunities and say no to the possibilities being presented to you. Different reasons, such as lack of interest, apathy, or being too busy, are behind these denials. You may be going within to reflect and realign yourself before committing to something new. This card shows boredom and a lack of engagement. Disconnecting yourself from new experiences due to past traumas is also a possibility.

REVERSED KEY WORDS: Realignment, Withdrawal, Going Within, Initiative

Reversed Meaning

You are removing yourself from the outside world and going within to focus on your needs and reassess yourself when the Four of Cups is reversed. You are spending time being introspective and working on aligning to what feels right. Challenges seem impossible to overcome because you are feeling uninspired and disheartened. This card reversed asks you to open yourself up to others instead of closing yourself off from fear of hurt.

Love and Relationships

For those looking for new relationships, opportunities are being ignored, and there is an air of boredom or indifference. You are not ready to seriously seek a new partner and/or can't be bothered right now. Current relationships may need renewal and excitement to combat feeling a lack of interest and dwindled romance.

Career and Wealth

Your career no longer provides excitement and holds your interest with the Four of Cups. You are feeling stagnant and distracted when it comes to work. Distraction is taking your focus away from projects and affecting you negatively. Contemplation is needed to get past this. Money may cause frustration when you focus on what you lack.

Success and Happiness

For success and happiness to be possible when the Four of Cups appears, you need to reassess your situation and spend time thinking about what will make you happy. Think outside the box and be open to opportunities you may not have considered. Try shaking up your normal routine.

Wild Card

There are times when the Four of Cups shows you that your ideas or actions are still encouraged, but it's not the time to act on them just yet. This card suggests you wait before agreeing to move forward and spend time contemplating to see whether you feel aligned with your ideas.

FIVE OF CUPS

5 OF CUPS

NUMEROLOGY: Loss

ASTROLOGY: Scorpio

ELEMENT: Water

COLORS: Black, Yellow, Brown, Blue, Red

SYMBOLS: Cloak, Fallen Cups, Bridge, River

UPRIGHT KEY WORDS: Disappointment, Dejected, Gloomy, Regret, Failure, Mourning

Upright Meaning

Disappointing situations consume you with the Five of Cups. You find yourself wallowing in sadness and regret, unable to move forward. You are focusing on the upsets of the past and are not seeing all that you still have to look forward to or appreciate. This card is steeped in negativity and dejection, with an air of gloom and mourning. Release yourself from the past to stop feeling like a victim.

REVERSED KEY WORDS: Self-Forgiveness, Hope, Rekindling, Released Pain

Reversed Meaning

You may be hiding your emotional pain from others and feeling as though you have failed yourself. This card reversed speaks of seeking self-forgiveness and releasing the stored pain. The Five of Cups reversed can indicate a new sense of hope or a rekindling of connections with others. Pain and suffering is coming to an end.

Love and Relationships

Relationships may be experiencing a time of sadness or disappointment. The Five of Cups brings emotional grief in love, and you may be mourning if there's been a breakup. You are experiencing relationship tension and disagreements. Hope is not lost, however, and good things can still come from the upset.

Career and Wealth

Financial stress and monetary loss are likely with the Five of Cups. Even so, there are ways to rebuild your resources, and this card encourages you to do just that. There may be setbacks in your career or disappointment from delays and loss. Hard transitions are occurring, including the potential for job loss.

Success and Happiness

Grief and sadness from emotional baggage are weighing you down. To achieve success and happiness, release any anger or frustration and find forgiveness for yourself and others. Heal your emotions to clear your obstacles.

Wild Card

The Five of Cups teaches you to shift your thinking in situations to be able to focus on your new goals. Taking hard times of sadness and using them to work on yourself can help move you forward. You are reminded to have gratitude and be aware of your many blessings.

6 OF CUPS

NUMEROLOGY: **Compassion**

ASTROLOGY: **Scorpio**

ELEMENT: **Water**

COLORS: **Yellow, Red, Blue, Green, White**

SYMBOLS: **Flowers, Children, Pedestal**

Upright Meaning

Memories from your youth are coming to the surface as you reminisce about your childhood. These reminders bring you joy, and you may reconnect with someone from your past. The Six of Cups finds you in a more cooperative place with others, where there is balance, understanding, and a sense of giving without expectation. You are invited to connect to your inner child and experience innocence and joy. Be playful and carefree, as you were when you were a child.

REVERSED KEY WORDS: Lacking Joy, Stuck in the Past, Understanding

Reversed Meaning

Staying stuck in the past and relying on old memories to bring you joy becomes problematic with the Six of Cups reversed. You are not being present and allowing new opportunities. Situations from the past need to be forgiven and released. This card reversed signifies you have become disconnected from joy and happiness, and you need to reconnect with your inner child.

Love and Relationships

Single people will find themselves reconnecting with a former lover or someone from their past. Remembering the past is bringing you comfort now. Those in relationships are encouraged to reflect on happy moments from the past to get through rough times together. The past can help shape the future of your relationship.

Career and Wealth

Monetary gifts are being given to you as a financial resource. This is likely coming from your family. Alternatively, you may be giving back to them. Your career will benefit from looking to the past to see where adjustments may be needed or to reinspire you on your work path.

Success and Happiness

You may be receiving charitable acts of compassion or gifts from others in your life. The Six of Cups is a happy card of good blessings for your future. Reconnecting to the joy and simplicity of your childhood is recommended to align you with prosperity and positivity.

Wild Card

The Six of Cups can refer to literal children in your life. It is an opportunity to learn from young people and experience the world from their perspective. This card teaches you to reconnect with the magic and wonder of life. Additionally, the Six of Cups can indicate a pregnancy or a situation involving siblings.

7 OF CUPS

NUMEROLOGY: **Reflection**

ASTROLOGY: **Scorpio**

ELEMENT: **Water**

COLORS: **Gray, Blue, Green, Red, Yellow**

SYMBOLS: **Wreath, Jewels, Snake, Dragon, Clouds, Castle, Head, Cloth**

Upright Meaning

The Seven of Cups revolves around fantasy and overthinking situations. You fantasize about things you would like for yourself but never take action to get them. Bringing things to fruition is a challenge, as you lose focus and become caught up in confusion. Choices and opportunities are being presented to you, and they have you overwhelmed. You are caught up in unrealistic thoughts or illusions about the reality of these choices, making the decision more difficult.

REVERSED KEY WORDS: Expressing Dreams, Making Choices, Decisive, Unveiling, Alignment

Reversed Meaning

You are making choices with clarity and discernment when the Seven of Cups is reversed. You decide based on what feels right to you, not the people around you. Sharing your dreams and ideas is common with this reversal. The veil has lifted, and you see clearly what you want. Your plans are falling into alignment after you have reevaluated all of your options and chosen what feels best.

Love and Relationships

There are choices to be made about whom to enter into a relationship with. You may have several suitors or have to decide between love and a family, career, or other scenario. If you're in a relationship, you may be faced with decisions that could affect the future of your union. Weigh your options carefully.

Career and Wealth

Your finances can benefit from a reassessment of your financial standing. There are many routes to go, so the Seven of Cups invites you to think things over. Your career is giving you different options to consider about how you will move forward. Several new paths are being presented.

Success and Happiness

Clear the clutter in your head to pave the way to success and happiness. You are overwhelming yourself with fantasy and unrealistic prospects. This is holding you back from attaining joy. The Seven of Cups suggests you take action after contemplation to bring in good fortune.

Wild Card

Action is now necessary to fulfill your goals. This card finds you hopping from one idea to the next without ever finishing any of your projects. It is time to choose a plan that you feel good about and get started. Stop going back and forth and put your dreams into motion.

EIGHT OF CUPS

8 OF CUPS

NUMEROLOGY: **Progression**

ASTROLOGY: **Pisces**

ELEMENT: **Water**

COLORS: **Blue, Yellow, Green, Red, Black**

SYMBOLS: **Arranged Cups, Staff, Water, Mountains, Moon**

Upright Meaning

This card depicts the dark night of the soul, a time when you are feeling unfulfilled, disappointed, and eager to escape your surroundings. This is a time for some deep and serious soul searching. The Eight of Cups symbolizes walking away from what no longer serves you or moving on from hurtful or confusing situations. You feel as if something is missing, so you must put the past behind you and allow your newfound wisdom to guide you forward.

REVERSED KEY WORDS: Satisfaction, Staying, Fulfillment, Involvement

Reversed Meaning

You have found the fulfillment you were seeking when the Eight of Cups is reversed. You have thought things over and decided that staying in a situation is in your best interest. Satisfaction and contentment have risen to the surface, and you have rejoined social interactions, becoming involved once again with life.

Love and Relationships

Something is missing in your relationship, and you are asking yourself deep questions. The Eight of Cups has you wondering what you need to feel gratified with your partner. The pros and cons of staying are being weighed, and your happiness may be found when you walk away.

Career and Wealth

You may need to leave something behind in order to move ahead financially. Bigger purchases are better left waiting for another time. Your career is no longer providing fulfillment, and time away offers a chance to regroup. Totally stepping away from the position is a possibility.

Success and Happiness

Take some time away to clear your head, lift your spirits, and bring back feelings of contentment. A break from your troubles will help you bring in more prosperity and joy, according to the Eight of Cups. It is time to leave the worries behind.

Wild Card

You may be involved in a situation that is causing you great emotional distress or problems. Serious concerns are being avoided or ignored. You refuse to address these problems and communicate your needs. This card invites you to work through these concerns and reflect on what will help you through.

9 OF CUPS

NUMEROLOGY: **Attainment**

ASTROLOGY: **Pisces**

ELEMENT: **Water**

COLORS: **Yellow, Blue, Red, Brown, White**

SYMBOLS: **Curved Arch, Bench, Crossed Arms, Smile**

Upright Meaning

Contentment reaches across all areas of your life when the Nine of Cups appears. Your desires are being fulfilled, and your wishes have been granted. What you seek is on the way. Satisfaction is found with this card, along with abundance. You are welcome to splurge on life's pleasures and really enjoy yourself now. Show gratitude to continue attracting the things you wish for in life.

REVERSED KEY WORDS: Smugness, Unfulfilled Wish, Materialistic, Overindulgence, Discontent

Reversed Meaning

Part of you feels as if something is missing, despite having everything you have wanted. The Nine of Cups reversed reveals a lack of satisfaction in your life. Something you have been hoping for did not come to fruition, and you are feeling the disappointment. There are times when this reversal indicates materialism and excessive indulgence. You are cautioned not to become too smug when things are going well.

Love and Relationships

This card is a good sign when you're looking for love, indicating that your wish will soon be granted. Happy social settings amplify your chances for finding romance with the Nine of Cups. Relationships are full of cheer, and you are feeling more closely drawn together with your partner.

Career and Wealth

Career advancement, raises, and promotions are possible with the Nine of Cups. Now is the time to act on your desires at work, as it is likely you will get your way. Your hard work is recognized. You are in a good place financially and may even receive extra funds.

Success and Happiness

The Nine of Cups depicts your wishes coming true and is a very positive card to receive in readings for success and happiness. Your desires are being fulfilled and a place of contentment is likely. Joy and stability stem from this card, radiating with positive energy.

Wild Card

You are reminded that good times can last only for so long, and the comfortable feeling you are experiencing can be fleeting. The Nine of Cups emphasizes enjoying the present moment and counting your blessings, because gratification can come and go. Cherish the happy moments.

TEN OF CUPS

10 OF CUPS

NUMEROLOGY: Completion

ASTROLOGY: Pisces

ELEMENT: Water

COLORS: Red, Purple, Blue, Green, Yellow

SYMBOLS: Rainbow, House, Hill, Children, Outstretched Arms

UPRIGHT KEY WORDS: Happiness, Fulfillment, Appreciation, Harmony, Alignment, Happy Relationships

Upright Meaning

Love and harmony shine through with the Ten of Cups. This is especially true for relationships and family. Joy, contentment, and emotional satisfaction have been attained or are on the way. Everything is smooth sailing and harmonious. Strong connections and states of peaceful bliss are recognized with this card.

REVERSED KEY WORDS: Dissatisfaction, Threatened Happiness, Relationship Problems, Lack of Appreciation, Misalignment, Disconnection

Reversed Meaning

Happiness may be threatened when the Ten of Cups is reversed. You may be having struggles in your relationship or feeling unsatisfied. The lack of harmony and the disconnect have you challenged when it comes to communicating and feeling balanced. Personal values are not aligning, and there is a lack of appreciation. Reversed, this card suggests you are neglecting your family and spirituality for more material things.

Love and Relationships

Relationship commitments are increasing, such as a proposal, marriage, or meeting each other's families. You and your partner are experiencing feelings of calm, tranquility, and bliss. If you are looking for love, this card reveals that your next relationship holds great and lasting potential.

Career and Wealth

Finances are stable, and you have enough to feel comfortable. Your career is bringing you joy, along with opportunities to grow and create. The workplace feels harmonious, and you have a sense of belonging. Your job offers a happy work-life balance, allowing more time for family.

Success and Happiness

The Ten of Cups is a very positive card to receive in readings, indicating peace, love, harmony, and happiness. Success and achievement are possible, and you should start seeing changes for the better soon. Good luck is approaching, leaving you with a sense of stability.

Wild Card

Intuition is an aspect of this card, inviting you to follow your inner guidance to find states of harmony. Release control and allow your feelings to direct you to new opportunities or steer you away from situations that may not benefit you. Following your heart more will lead you to lasting contentment.

PAGE OF CUPS

PAGE OF CUPS

NUMEROLOGY: **Balance**

ASTROLOGY: **Pisces**

ELEMENT: **Water**

COLORS: **Yellow, Blue, Red, Brown, White**

SYMBOLS: **Fish, Land, Water**

Upright Meaning

The Page of Cups represents an intuitive and creative person or a youthful and curious energy. This card is about new and unexpected opportunities that are creative in nature and about the way you choose to express yourself. Your curiosity and open-minded outlook allow you to discover yourself and reach new potentials. Anything is possible and your intuition plays an important role. Be aware of signs and messages to guide you to happiness and alignment.

REVERSED KEY WORDS: Pressure, Intuitive Doubt, Blocked Creativity

Reversed Meaning

You are experiencing an obstruction when it comes to expressing your creativity. This block has you withdrawing from sharing your ideas and projects with others until you are able to make progress. You are reluctant to accept new projects due to self-doubt and a disconnect from your intuition. There is a need to reconnect with your instinct and creative expression.

Love and Relationships

You may find a new partner who is in touch with their emotions and creative side. For those in relationships, you are viewing your partner with a sense of awe and newness. You feel fascinated by and appreciative of your lover.

Career and Wealth

The daydreams you have about your career goals want to be put into action. The Page of Cups suggests you will thrive in a creative and expressive work field and encourages you to follow your dreams. You may have unrealistic financial goals, so focus on what is actually achievable.

Success and Happiness

Positive news is likely when the Page of Cups comes up in tarot readings. Your intuition has you connected to your inner guidance, and this steers you toward fulfilling your dreams. Embrace your dreamy and sensitive nature to allow more prosperity to flow into your life.

Wild Card

When this card arrives in readings, sometimes it means you have to think outside the box in your life. You may need to find different ways to communicate or approach situations. The Page of Cups can also indicate good news and messages arriving, such as surprise announcements, projects, or relationships.

KNIGHT OF CUPS

KNIGHT OF CUPS

NUMEROLOGY: **Creation**

ASTROLOGY: **Pisces**

ELEMENT: **Water**

COLORS: **Blue, White, Gold**

SYMBOLS: **Fish, Wings, River, Armor, Horse**

UPRIGHT KEY WORDS: Romance, Charm, Artistic, Creativity, Devotion, Daydreamer

Upright Meaning

The Knight depicts a slow and dreamy romance, and the emotion is full of creativity, compassion, and fantasy. An appreciation of beauty and imagination may indicate a proposal or a romantic gesture. Decisions are often made from the heart. The Knight of Cups also shows a desire for action on new creative ideas, passions, or projects.

REVERSED KEY WORDS: Unrealistic, Temperamental, Self-Absorbed, Irresponsible, Impractical, Trickery

Reversed Meaning

The Knight reversed shows the need to be practical when it comes to dreams and goals. Plans may be chaotic, because the Knight is caught up in the excitement of ideas without contemplating reality. In reversal, the Knight may depict a misleading, unpredictable, or manipulative person.

Love and Relationships

The Knight of Cups can indicate a romantic gesture, a deeper commitment, or a marriage proposal. This card brings sensitivity, compassion, and emotional connections. Those not in a relationship may expect a charming person, with intense attraction and flirting. The Knight suggests feelings of love and affection.

Career and Wealth

When it comes to career and wealth, there is often an artistic element, with new projects or ideas being created. The Knight represents the ability to solve problems related to work with compassion. Job prospects, offers, and finances are all usually opportunities with positive outcomes when this card appears.

Success and Happiness

The Knight of Cups often appears as a positive card, full of virtue and heartfelt intentions. To achieve success, one must sort through their many ideas before taking action. The Knight stresses the importance of following your passions to allow harmony in your life.

Wild Card

The Knight of Cups signifies growing intuition and insight. A person may be recognizing messages through synchronicity or learning to trust their instinct more. This card is like a nod from the universe acknowledging alignment on one's path. The Knight may also show upcoming travel or holidays with loved ones.

QUEEN OF CUPS

QUEEN OF CUPS

NUMEROLOGY: **Stability**

ASTROLOGY: **Gemini**

ELEMENT: **Water**

COLORS: **Blue, Yellow, Green, Red, Purple**

SYMBOLS: **Sea, Closed Cup, Throne, Fish**

Upright Meaning

The Queen of Cups overflows with nurturing and loving energy. You are supportive, heartfelt, and compassionate. Others turn to you for empathy. Your intuition allows you to tune into the needs of other people. This card reveals a highly creative side and an emotional stability with a healing nature.

REVERSED KEY WORDS: Insincerity, Emotional Disconnect, Temperamental, Self-Care, Codependent

Reversed Meaning

You are spending so much time caring for others that you have neglected yourself. This lack of self-care leaves you emotionally disconnected to the point of no longer expressing genuine emotions. Reversed, the Queen of Cups shows that self-love and being self-nurturing are needed right now. Perhaps you have become codependent with another person as a result of overcaring and giving too much of yourself.

Love and Relationships

People will be attracted to how kind and supportive you are, making way for potential love interests. Intuition is important—be sure not to take on emotionally dependent partners with your caring nature. In relationships, expect your love connection to deepen significantly.

Career and Wealth

Your kind heart has you offering financial support to those in need. You recognize that money isn't everything and place value on nonmaterial items. Your career is fulfilling, and there is nurturing guidance being offered at your workplace. At times, you may be the one guiding and caring for staff.

Success and Happiness

Support may be offered to you as a way to help you achieve your success. The Queen of Cups often portrays positive outcomes in these scenarios, and there is an emphasis on connecting to your emotions and instinct to bring in what you would like to manifest.

Wild Card

The Queen of Cups shows that you work best when you trust your intuition and navigate with your heart, as opposed to your head. Creative projects benefit from inner knowing and following your instinct. You are invited to feel all of your emotions fully and express them through your creations.

KING OF CUPS

KING OF CUPS

NUMEROLOGY: Change

ASTROLOGY: Scorpio

ELEMENT: Water

COLORS: Blue, Yellow, Red, Green, Gray

SYMBOLS: Throne, Tunic, Cape, Fish Amulet, Scepter, Sea, Waves

Upright Meaning

Emotional maturity is predominant with the King of Cups. You act from a place of emotional balance and mastery, having worked through your feelings and accepted the challenges thrown your way. Creativity and successful achievements are portrayed with this card. There is a level-headed balance between head and heart, and the King acts with tact in even the most difficult situations.

REVERSED KEY WORDS: Self-Compassion, Insecurity, Anger, Uncontrolled Emotions, Blocked Creativity

Reversed Meaning

You are working on mastering your emotions. The goal is to gain emotional self-control and maturity. You may be easily triggered and have upsets and outbursts that need attention. Try to find balance and self-compassion. Be mindful not to repress your emotions and withdraw from others when you are triggered.

Love and Relationships

Your relationship benefits by balancing both head and heart. Emotional maturity and calm responses to conflict keep a steady balance. The King of Cups portrays practical but compassionate romance. Those seeking partnership are asked to blend logic with emotion. This card shows a peaceful relationship.

Career and Wealth

Your career needs a balance between emotion and practicality. A wise and compassionate mentor will help you grow in your work. This balance and guidance help you attain an emotionally satisfying career. Your finances are stable, and larger transactions call for logical caution before proceeding.

Success and Happiness

The King of Cups is a positive card to receive when it comes to success and happiness. You are likely to receive what you are seeking and will be able to manifest prosperity. This card speaks of emotional fulfillment and accomplishment. You can expect to flourish.

Wild Card

You may have a masculine energy, father-like figure (not necessarily male) in your life to guide you. This person acts as a mentor or a coach, showing you how to balance your emotions with patience and understanding. Your feelings are influenced by this figure, and at times you are the one in this mentor role.

CHAPTER 8

THE MINOR ARCANA: PENTACLES

IN THIS CHAPTER WE'LL DIVE DEEPLY into the Minor Arcana suit of Pentacles and learn what kinds of insights the Pentacles offer in tarot readings. A pentacle is a talisman on which a magical symbol is drawn; in tarot it is often depicted as a disk with a pentagram on it. Pentacles reveal the more material side of life, such as home, career, finance, and health. Pentacles represent earthly elements and our exterior surroundings. These cards can speak of prosperity and manifestation. This chapter explains the key words and meanings for each card in the suit, from the Ace (which is one) through the King of Pentacles.

ACE OF PENTACLES

ACE OF PENTACLES

NUMEROLOGY: Opportunity

ASTROLOGY: Saturn

ELEMENT: Earth

COLORS: Yellow, Green, Red, Gray, Blue

SYMBOLS: Cloud, Coin, Hand, Garden, Path, Archway, Flowers

UPRIGHT KEY WORDS: Abundance, Manifestation, Career Opportunity, Successful Venture, Tangible Beginning

Upright Meaning

Material elements are being presented as new opportunities or beginnings. Prospects regarding career, wealth, health, or other material opportunities are being offered to you. The Ace of Pentacles points to the manifestation of your goals. This card indicates the potential for abundance in your life, finding you in the early stages of a new venture. It signifies that hard work is needed to bring your dreams to fruition, and you are at a promising starting point.

REVERSED KEY WORDS: Financial Insecurity, Material Loss, Poor Planning, Lost Opportunity

Reversed Meaning

Opportunities have been offered to you, yet you are hesitating to take action. There may be a career or financial opportunity that you are reluctant to proceed on when the Ace of Pentacles is reversed. Unexpected delays or unfulfilled opportunities with new ventures are likely with this card, along with financial instability. Your planning needs to be revised to get you back on track.

Love and Relationships

Stable and reliable relationships are connected to the Ace of Pentacles. Your partner is loyal and giving with this card, and each of you contributes to the relationship. There is a feeling of prosperity and appreciation. If you are seeking love, this card suggests you build a practical foundation for yourself before committing.

Career and Wealth

Promotions or new careers appear for your consideration. New opportunities with potential for abundance are on the way with the Ace of Pentacles. This card speaks of a time of positivity in your career and opportunities to grow your finances.

Success and Happiness

The Ace of Pentacles indicates improvements and good signs for your success and happiness. There are new opportunities for positivity with this card. New motivations and inspirations will keep you going toward prosperity. Expect a windfall, along with feelings of stability.

Wild Card

There are times when the Ace of Pentacles speaks beyond the materialistic to achieving abundance across the board. You may find yourself in a prosperous place with your life, your career, finances, health, and relationships. This card shows you are likely to soon start thriving in all areas.

TWO OF PENTACLES

2 OF PENTACLES

NUMEROLOGY: **Balance**

ASTROLOGY: **Capricorn**

ELEMENT: **Earth**

COLORS: **Red, Blue, Yellow, Green, Brown**

SYMBOLS: **Infinity Symbol, Ship, Ocean Waves**

Upright Meaning

Juggling priorities is the theme of the Two of Pentacles. When this card appears, you are filling several roles in your life and trying to multitask. You are finding a balance between different areas, such as career and home, but are close to your breaking point. Your time and energy must be managed, and prioritizing is important at this time. Stay aware of your ongoing commitments and deadlines so they do not become lost in the shuffle.

REVERSED KEY WORDS: Overwhelmed, Disorganized, Overextended

Reversed Meaning

You have spread yourself too thin and are starting to feel the consequences of overextending yourself. Your commitments are being neglected due to the lack of balance, and you are struggling to keep up. Reversed, the Two of Pentacles speaks of disorganization and a lack of prioritizing. At times, you may be neglecting loved ones by focusing too much on one area.

Love and Relationships

Life is hectic, and you are trying to juggle everything at once. This is putting a strain on your relationship. The Two of Pentacles reminds you to pay attention to your partner and their needs. People looking for new relationships are advised to prioritize and get organized before starting anything new.

Career and Wealth

You are being assigned project after project, leaving you overwhelmed. Balance is important in your career, and this card highlights your resourcefulness. Manage your time and responsibilities carefully. Finances are unstable, so juggle accordingly. Be flexible in how you manage your money.

Success and Happiness

Success and happiness come after you work on finding balance and harmony within the different areas of your life with the Two of Pentacles. Focus on organizing your life so you can start to feel stability. You are asked to take a steady approach to achieve prosperity.

Wild Card

This card encourages you to be flexible and adaptable. Patience is often required with the Two of Pentacles, as is allowing yourself to loosen control of your regimen. As you strive to achieve balance, you may be causing yourself disharmony by trying to fight against your needs and not going with the flow.

THREE OF PENTACLES

3 OF PENTACLES

NUMEROLOGY: Growth

ASTROLOGY: Capricorn

ELEMENT: Earth

COLORS: Red, Black, Gray, Yellow, Blue

SYMBOLS: Triangle, Rose, Celtic Cross, Robe, Thorny Crown, Yellow Apron, Violets

Upright Meaning

The Three of Pentacles emerges when it is time for you to take your skills and collaborate with others on projects and ideas. This card shows that you have something to offer others while learning from them as well. Everyone brings something to the table in this group effort, and you have been making progress in your endeavors. Your creation is in the early stages, and you are continuing to learn and grow.

REVERSED KEY WORDS: No Ambition, Work Problems, No Cooperation, Poor Performance

Reversed Meaning

There is an imbalance among the people you are working with on projects and ideas. The lack of harmony is causing misalignment, and the project is now far from completion. Reversed, this card reveals that planning and cooperation are needed. You may be working below your skill level and feeling a lack of drive. If you are working alone, this card invites you to ask others for help.

Love and Relationships

Couples are encouraged to do fun or creative projects together, work on their home as a team, or collaborate in some way. This encourages a stronger bond and injects more fun into the relationship. This card suggests that single people will find partnership through work gatherings or hobbies they enjoy.

Career and Wealth

Your finances may need to come together a bit more, and the Three of Pentacles suggests finding a financial advisor. Career projects benefit from collaboration and teamwork. Look for new ideas from others, and continue learning and building experience.

Success and Happiness

The effort and dedication you have been putting into achieving your dreams is starting to pay off and turn into something positive. Keep going, as prosperity is soon approaching. Reach out to others for support or guidance along the way.

Wild Card

This card validates that you have the skills and resources to implement everything you have learned to accomplish your goals. You are on the right track and headed in the right direction. You have the necessary resources and are capable of bringing everything together.

4 OF PENTACLES

NUMEROLOGY: **Planning**

ASTROLOGY: **Capricorn**

ELEMENT: **Earth**

COLORS: **Red, Black, Blue, Yellow, Gray**

SYMBOLS: **Stool, City Buildings**

UPRIGHT KEY WORDS: Conservation, Security, Holding Tightly, Saving Finances, Material Possessions

Upright Meaning

Money and finances are often centered around the Four of Pentacles. Your wealth is achieved through careful planning and conservation, but you come from a place of need. You focus on saving money at the expense of happiness. Material possessions are where you place your self-value. At times, this card suggests that you manage your money carefully and save your earnings.

REVERSED KEY WORDS: Letting Go, Lacking Structure, Financial Loss, Greed, Excessive Spending

Reversed Meaning

Material possessions have lost their emphasis in your life, and money is starting to loosen its grip on you. Reversed, this card can point to financial loss or a lack of structure when spending money. You may be spending excessively to the point of greed. At times, the reversal shows a need to conserve energy and ground yourself to feel stable.

Love and Relationships

Those seeking a partner must resolve past relationship trauma and resentments before discovering new love. The Four of Pentacles suggests couples who wrestle with insecurities and possessiveness. Relationships may have clingy or suffocating attributes, and issues must be faced. Examine all fears and work through them.

Career and Wealth

Group projects at work are challenging, leaving you feeling guarded and on edge. You are reluctant to share your ideas and prefer to work alone. This card can indicate stability at work, yet it is an unfulfilling career. Financially, you are being extra conservative and very focused on money.

Success and Happiness

Old baggage and the past can stand in the way of finding success and happiness. The Four of Pentacles encourages you to let go of old patterns and behaviors to make way for new beginnings. Divert your focus from materialism to more meaningful attributes in your life.

Wild Card

Something is holding you back from happiness, and the only way to be free is to let go. This card indicates a need to release what is compromising your happiness. You are clinging tightly to what no longer serves you, and the Four of Pentacles invites you to loosen your grip.

FIVE OF PENTACLES

5 OF PENTACLES

NUMEROLOGY: Conflict

ASTROLOGY: Taurus

ELEMENT: Earth

COLORS: Black, White, Blue, Red, Yellow

SYMBOLS: Church, Storm, Crutches, Shawl

Upright Meaning

Hard times are here, predominantly involving material possessions, career, or finances. Monetary loss and poverty are possible with the Five of Pentacles. This card also signifies feeling lonely, isolated, or left out. There is a feeling of being without help or hope. However, help is nearby and you can be supported, but you must look up from your problems to notice it. The reassuring aspect to this card is that the struggle is temporary.

REVERSED KEY WORDS: Recovery, Relief, Support, Renewed Faith, Positive Turn

Reversed Meaning

Reversed, the Five of Pentacles can be a welcome card, as it indicates hard times are almost over and troubles are lifting. Career opportunities, monetary support, and other forms of help are appearing. This card reversed portrays a restoration of faith and hope. The struggle is ending. At times, you may be in need of spiritual alignment as opposed to focusing on the material. You are encouraged to find more meaningful fulfillment in your life.

Love and Relationships

You may be feeling very lonely and desolate when it comes to finding a relationship. The Five of Pentacles reveals a doomed outlook for those seeking love. Couples are likely experiencing feelings of disconnection and loneliness toward each other, as if they are lacking an emotional bond.

Career and Wealth

Money is very tight right now, and there is financial hardship. This card asks you to look for help and support if you are in need. Your career is struggling, and the workplace may have you feeling left out and lacking. At this point, the situation may warrant searching for a new job.

Success and Happiness

The Five of Pentacles often reflects periods of difficulty and lack. You are struggling to get by and may be feeling quite isolated. The situation feels hopeless, but know that with this card also comes the reminder that your hardships are temporary. Things can always change for the better.

Wild Card

Fear and focusing on the negative come up with this card. You are feeling that everything in your life is lacking, keeping yourself in a loop of scarcity. You constantly focus on what you perceive as wrong, so you are encouraged to shift your mindset to one of gratitude.

SIX OF PENTACLES

6 OF PENTACLES

NUMEROLOGY: Compassion

ASTROLOGY: Taurus

ELEMENT: Earth

COLORS: Red, Blue, Yellow, Green, Gray

SYMBOLS: Scale, Coins, Robe, Cloak

Upright Meaning

Generosity and sharing your wealth are key meanings of the Six of Pentacles. You may be well off financially or just enjoy helping others, but when this card appears, it shows you are giving to and assisting others. At times, what you offer may be time, energy, or support, as opposed to tangible relief. This card indicates that your good service will come back to you in kind, and your efforts do not go unnoticed.

REVERSED KEY WORDS: Financial Loss, Self-Help, Equal Distribution, Owing Money

Reversed Meaning

The need for self-care is evident when the Six of Pentacles is reversed. It is time to spend some money, time, or indulgence on yourself for a change. You are so busy giving to others that you have neglected your own needs. At times, this card can reflect financial loss or a period when you have debts to pay off. The Six of Pentacles, when reversed, can also indicate an equal sharing between you and other people.

Love and Relationships

Your partner is very generous and supportive of you with this card. Emotional and financial needs are taken care of while you focus on self-growth. The Six of Pentacles reminds you to show appreciation to keep the relationship balanced. Those seeking love are encouraged to share their time and energy accordingly.

Career and Wealth

Stay alert for a mentor entering your life to help you in your career. This person is generous with their time and willing to help you get ahead. It is possible that bonuses or promotions are in order. Financially, you are doing well enough to help others or are about to receive a loan.

Success and Happiness

You can expect a boost or shift toward success and happiness with the Six of Pentacles. This card encourages you to give what you hope to receive. Reach out to others for support and be mindful to stay gracious and full of gratitude.

Wild Card

The Six of Pentacles can recommend that you become open to receiving charity or help from others. This card asks you to seek support or accept gifts from those around you. You will be able to give back once you become more stable financially or in terms of your energy.

SEVEN OF PENTACLES

7 OF PENTACLES

NUMEROLOGY: Reflection

ASTROLOGY: Taurus

ELEMENT: Earth

COLORS: Orange, Blue, Red, Purple, Green

SYMBOLS: Shovel, Crops, Garden, Mountains

Upright Meaning

You are putting in much effort and hard work toward your long-term goals. The vision you have is far in the distance, but you are working every day to get to the finish line. The Seven of Pentacles reminds you that the time you are spending will pay off in the long run. You are also encouraged to step back and reassess your progress. Appreciate your efforts so far, and adjust what is not working.

REVERSED KEY WORDS: New Project, Giving Up, Limited Vision, Delayed Success

Reversed Meaning

Focus is lacking with the Seven of Pentacles reversed. You are all over the place and not seeing your vision clearly. This card reveals that you may have given up too soon and are dropping one project for another. Your success is limited or delayed when this card is reversed, and you are encouraged to realize when it is time to change direction and try something new. Adjust your priorities so you start seeing a return on your hard work.

Love and Relationships

Friendships are likely to turn to romance over time with the Seven of Pentacles. Someone you consider a friend can become something more, offering a steady and long-term relationship. Those already paired up have to put more effort and work into their relationship to continue to grow.

Career and Wealth

You are making progress in your career. It may not feel this way, as results are very slow coming to fruition. The Seven of Pentacles reveals that hard work is paying off toward your big-picture goals. Evaluate your position to see whether you are happy staying the course. Finances are beginning to flourish.

Success and Happiness

Receiving the Seven of Pentacles in readings is a good sign that you are able to manifest your goals. For success and happiness, contemplate your situation and make adjustments as needed. Your hard work and efforts will pay off in a rewarding way.

Wild Card

Frustration can come up with the Seven of Pentacles. You have been working very hard for a long time and are still not seeing huge results. Fatigue and impatience are creeping in. This card reminds you to keep going and hold tight to your vision.

EIGHT OF PENTACLES

8 OF PENTACLES

NUMEROLOGY: **Attainment**

ASTROLOGY: **Virgo**

ELEMENT: **Earth**

COLORS: **Blue, Red, Brown, Yellow, Green**

SYMBOLS: **Nail, Bench, Town**

Upright Meaning

Skills are being mastered, and you are continuing to learn more about your craft. Your endeavors are being enhanced by an apprenticeship or further education. You have built a strong foundation, and now you are fine-tuning your skill set with the Eight of Pentacles. Progress is being made, and you have created structure. You are inspired to keep perfecting your craft in order to flourish. This card can also apply to the details of your life aside from work.

REVERSED KEY WORDS: Impatience, Shortcuts, Dissatisfaction, Self-Development, Misdirection

Reversed Meaning

When the Seven of Pentacles is reversed, it signifies the need for self-discipline and inner work. You are mastering your own development and working toward self-growth as a person. When it comes to your career or business endeavors, you have become impatient. You are not satisfied with the results, and the effort is not enjoyable to you. Corners are being cut as a result, and these shortcuts are having a negative impact. Your direction must be realigned to see progress.

Love and Relationships

Appreciating yourself, your partner, and your relationship are aspects of the Eight of Pentacles. You have to be patient and put in the effort to grow your partnership. If you are seeking romance, this card asks you to appreciate all you have to offer another person.

Career and Wealth

Financial rewards, such as a bonus or promotion, are likely. Your hard work and money management are paying off. The Eight of Pentacles finds you dedicated to your career. The improvement and growth shown are moving you toward success. Continue to learn and find mentors to hone your craft.

Success and Happiness

You have been working hard to achieve success and happiness. The Eight of Pentacles reveals that your efforts and diligence will come to fruition soon. Abundance and rewards for your dedication are likely with this card. Expect growth and movement forward toward your vision.

Wild Card

This card can be seen as a nod of encouragement and a reminder to stay focused on your path. The Eight of Pentacles shows that patience is necessary to reach your goal, along with dedication. If you are not currently pursuing a craft, this card urges you to reflect on a path that fulfills you.

NINE OF PENTACLES

9 OF PENTACLES

NUMEROLOGY: Fulfillment

ASTROLOGY: Virgo

ELEMENT: Earth

COLORS: Yellow, Red, Green, Blue, Purple

SYMBOLS: Robe, Grapes, Garden, Falcon, Tree

UPRIGHT KEY WORDS: Prosperity, Abundance, Self-Sufficient, Achievement, Independence, Decadence

Upright Meaning

You are in a successful, stable place in your life. The Nine of Pentacles portrays accomplishment and prosperity. This card symbolizes abundance, and you are likely very independent. Your hard work has led you to this point of luxury, and it is time for you to enjoy your efforts. Your financial freedom offers you feelings of stability.

REVERSED KEY WORDS: Undisciplined, Feeling Unworthy, Dependent, Overworked, Instability

Reversed Meaning

You question your self-worth and value, as you feel undeserving of all you are working toward. You feel as if you are not good enough or worth the extra effort, so you undersell your services and downplay your skills. Reversed, this card may show that you lack financial independence or stability. You are working hard but not seeing results, due to a lack of discipline.

Love and Relationships

Single people are enjoying the luxuries of life and the freedom that comes with them. Your independence and high standards attract others for possible romance. Relationships have a healthy balance of partnership and independence, and you may be investing in your home together with this card.

Career and Wealth

Money matters are secure and prosperous with the Nine of Pentacles. Achievements and success are found in your career, as your business flourishes from all your hard work. This card can suggest a vacation is warranted.

Success and Happiness

This is a welcome card of success and achievement, as well as abundance and good news. You will see the benefits of your efforts begin to show. This card emphasizes gratitude and paying it forward once you are in a place of accomplishment, continuing to evoke happiness and prosperity.

Wild Card

There are times when the Nine of Pentacles refers to your harmonic alignment with nature. You appreciate the beauty around you, the Earth, and the wonders of nature. The abundant energy suits you, and gardening or nature walks appeal to your interests.

10 OF PENTACLES

NUMEROLOGY: **Completion**

ASTROLOGY: **Virgo**

ELEMENT: **Earth**

COLORS: **Red, Blue, Brown, White, Green**

SYMBOLS: **White Hair, Robe, Dog**

Upright Meaning

After hard work and perseverance, you have reached a completion point in your life. You have achieved great security, success, and financial wealth. Your home life is stable and content, and the family is well taken care of. The Ten of Pentacles speaks of accomplishment and a place of abundance. A lasting foundation has been created with this card, and you find yourself sharing your blessings with others, such as family and friends.

REVERSED KEY WORDS: Family Conflict, Financial Failure, Lack of Security

Reversed Meaning

This card when reversed has you questioning the finer things in life and whether the pursuit of them really makes you happy. You are no longer interested in material wealth but rather quality time. On the home front, there may be a lack of harmony with family. Financial insecurity is possible, and you are lacking a stable foundation. Money may be tight, and you are experiencing setbacks in your life, such as in finances, career, family, or relationships.

Love and Relationships

Strong and happy relationships are evident with the Ten of Pentacles. There is both abundance and stability, as well as a possible milestone approaching, such as marriage. Those seeking partnership are interested in long-term relationships and secure partners. This card indicates the arrival of such a romance is likely.

Career and Wealth

You are establishing permanence in your career. Your job is secure and successful with the Ten of Pentacles. At times, this card shows your work to be family related. Financially, you may be receiving a large sum of money. Your income is in a good place, and you are saving for the future.

Success and Happiness

Long-term success and happiness seem steady and likely when the Ten of Pentacles shows up. You are supported by your family and experiencing harmony. You are manifesting your goals and on the way to fulfillment. This card reminds you to share your blessings with loved ones.

Wild Card

The Ten of Pentacles can portray the importance of family in your life. Your ancestry and heritage are very meaningful to you, and your loved ones are a happy part of your life. Heritage and family traditions are celebrated. Also, this card can refer to family inheritance.

PAGE OF PENTACLES

NUMEROLOGY: Choices

ASTROLOGY: Capricorn

ELEMENT: Earth

COLORS: Green, Red, Yellow, Brown, Blue

SYMBOLS: Tree, Flowers, Mountains, Field

Upright Meaning

Here you have the inspiration for the early stages of a venture or project. New beginnings are upon you with the Page of Pentacles, and you are working toward manifesting your vision. This card can reflect opportunities more material in nature, such as in your career, finances, projects, or health. There is much potential here, and you are encouraged to learn a new skill or become educated in an area of interest. Gain more experience to ensure success.

REVERSED KEY WORDS: Difficulty Learning, Mediocre Progress, Procrastination, Lost Opportunity

Reversed Meaning

You may be considering a new opportunity, but when the Page of Pentacles is reversed, you have yet to move forward. The idea is sitting with you while you consider the possibilities. Your skill set and experience are in question. Procrastination has halted opportunity. Or, your idea is stalled due to lack of progress.

Love and Relationships

You are in a dedicated and loyal relationship. The lack of excitement is balanced by the steady devotion; however, you are encouraged to be adventurous. If you are looking for love, you are likely to find a focused, driven, and practical partner when the Page of Pentacles appears.

Career and Wealth

Your career is presenting different opportunities to you, and furthering your education or skill set is recommended with this card. Build on your foundation to strengthen your position and be available to take on your dreams. Your finances will show a positive difference as the result of good budgeting and planning.

Success and Happiness

Continue to work on your personal growth and approach your situation with a youthful and vibrant outlook. Success and happiness come with dedication and learning when the Page of Pentacles emerges. Consider connecting to yourself in nature to regain balance and become grounded.

Wild Card

When the Page of Pentacles appears, the initial opportunity or idea is present, but the outcome is still dependent on your actions. To bring your dreams to life, planning and focus are necessary with this card. You are encouraged to stay grounded and realistic as you proceed.

KNIGHT OF PENTACLES

NUMEROLOGY: Growth

ASTROLOGY: Aquarius

ELEMENT: Earth

COLORS: Black, Red, Yellow, Silver, Green

SYMBOLS: Armor, Horse, Oak Leaves, Tree, Plowed Field

Upright Meaning

Hard work and effort will bring the results you desire. The Knight represents methodical dedication, and you are maintaining a steady pace toward your goal. The Knight of Pentacles symbolizes productivity and commitment. You stick to a routine, knowing what works for you to get the job done. The pace is slow and consistent, and you have meticulous focus that carries you through.

REVERSED KEY WORDS: Inactive, Inconsistent, Bored, Restless, No Progress, Self-Discipline

Reversed Meaning

Inconsistent practices leave you needing self-discipline to make progress. The Knight of Pentacles reversed shows you are not taking the proper actions to achieve results. You are feeling bored and restless, as if you are not moving forward. Your sense of adventure is missing, and the boredom of routine has left you without a creative spark. This card asks you to shake things up to get out of your rut.

Love and Relationships

This card reveals to those looking for love that a stable and committed partner is on the way. You likely will share the same goals, working together to create a future for yourselves. Current relationships are full of trust and reliability. Spontaneous actions are advised to break up the routine.

Career and Wealth

Careful planning and budgeting are advised for your finances. The Knight of Pentacles signifies future prosperity through regular saving. You are very ambitious in your career. Stay focused on your goals at work, as your drive and dedication are bound to lead to greater things.

Success and Happiness

One step at a time, through perseverance, your wishes are granted when the Knight of Pentacles is revealed. Stay the course and overcome your challenges with effort and dedication to ensure success and happiness in the long run. Your routine will help you navigate obstacles.

Wild Card

Boredom shows up with the Knight of Pentacles at times. You are going through the motions and dealing with the necessities of everyday life. Plodding along gets you through the routine. You stick to a conservative course in life, carefully planning every detail and step. Moderation helps you achieve success.

QUEEN OF PENTACLES

QUEEN OF PENTACLES

NUMEROLOGY: Stability

ASTROLOGY: Sagittarius

ELEMENT: Earth

COLORS: Green, Red, Blue, Yellow, Gray

SYMBOLS: Throne, Crown, Rabbit, Flowers

Upright Meaning

The Queen of Pentacles represents nurturing and a sensible way of approaching life. The Queen takes care of her loved ones with warmth and support while also tending to the home front. When this card appears, you balance work and home with ease. You are an abundant provider who offers security to your family. Compassion and practicality help you navigate challenges. You may also feel connected to nature and earthly environments.

REVERSED KEY WORDS: Aggressive, Family Imbalance, Closed Off, Greed, Self-Care

Reversed Meaning

Your family or home life has taken a back seat to your career needs. Reversed, the Queen of Pentacles shows you keeping your material gains for yourself and closing yourself off from loved ones. You may be having difficulty balancing your family and work, and your temperament has gone from nurturing to aggressive or irritable. At times, this card shows you caring for yourself, healing, and resting before caring for your loved ones again.

Love and Relationships

Your partner is kind, nurturing, and compassionate. The relationship is stable and abundant, and the Queen of Pentacles reveals a warm home environment. For people seeking companionship, this card shows a partner approaching who is committed and ambitious.

Career and Wealth

Your practical nature has you career-oriented and prosperous. Your talent paired with your sensibleness will benefit your career. A motherly mentor may guide you at this time, and collaborations will help you succeed. Finances are abundant and secure as a result of your hard work.

Success and Happiness

The Queen of Pentacles signifies fulfillment, and you are on track for abundance. Success and happiness are possible through practical measures. Your compassionate nature will support you in gaining prosperity. The Queen brings good news, joy, and warmth to your life in readings.

Wild Card

Motherly influences in your life can be represented through the Queen of Pentacles. A person like a mother to you (regardless of gender), such as a guide, mentor, or family member, is offering you support and care right now. Their nurturing tendencies will aid you, and you may recognize those attributes in yourself as well.

KING OF PENTACLES

NUMEROLOGY: **Change**

ASTROLOGY: **Capricorn**

ELEMENT: **Earth**

COLORS: **Purple, Red, Green, Blue, Black**

SYMBOLS: **Crown, Scepter, Grapes, Bull's Head**

Upright Meaning

Financial abundance and great success are attributes of the King of Pentacles. You are a leader and have achieved material security through your practical diligence. This card shows you sharing your wealth and leading others in a wise and fatherly manner. Abundance and success come easily to you, as you have a natural talent for business and managing others. You plan how to turn your visions into reality and work hard to get what you desire.

REVERSED KEY WORDS: Financial Worries, Insecurity, Not Satisfied, Stubborn

Reversed Meaning

Managing money and staying on top of your business ventures are challenging for you. Reversed, the King of Pentacles shows you struggling financially and without material security. This card can find you feeling dissatisfied, as if you never have enough. You may place too much emphasis on material possessions and money, negatively affecting your relationships. The King reversed can be stubborn at times, not willing to change his ways to find success.

Love and Relationships

Your partner is prosperous and dependable, offering stability in the relationship. Your life together is good, comfortable, and secure. If you are looking for love, a committed and successful partner is likely to appear.

Career and Wealth

You are now able to enjoy the financial rewards of your success and have reached a monetary milestone. Sharing the wealth is in your nature, and this card encourages splurging. Your career has reached a point of accomplishment, and you may find an experienced mentor at work to guide you further.

Success and Happiness

Your focus and dedication are leading you to a secure and successful place. This card is a good sign for happiness and abundance, and your life is likely to be enriched with blessings. The King of Pentacles is powerful and speaks of stability, well-being, and prosperity.

Wild Card

Projects, business ventures, or other endeavors have reached their final stage when the King of Pentacles emerges. You have achieved fulfillment and completed your goal. Your hard work has led to abundance in all areas of life, not just financially. Follow what works and continue manifesting your visions.

CHAPTER 9

THE MINOR ARCANA: SWORDS

NOW WE ARE READY TO EXPLORE what the Minor Arcana suit of Swords reveals in tarot readings. The Minor cards portray elements of our everyday life and how they affect the situations we are going through. Swords explain our mental state, such as our thoughts, beliefs, and intellect. Swords signify where we are on a conscious level. They revolve around action, power, change, or conflict. Logic and intelligence are common attributes of this suit. This chapter explains the key words and meanings for each card in the suit, from the Ace (which is one) through the King of Swords.

ACE OF SWORDS

ACE OF SWORDS

NUMEROLOGY: Potential

ASTROLOGY: Aquarius

ELEMENT: Air

COLORS: Gray, Blue, Purple, Green, Yellow

SYMBOLS: Crown, Cloud, Palm, Olive Branch, Sword, Mountains

UPRIGHT KEY WORDS: Clarity, New Ideas, Leap Forward, Progress, Success, Power

Upright Meaning

The Ace of Swords is a powerful card that appears when you are about to make a breakthrough or advance toward a new opportunity. You are on the verge of clarity and are about to have an epiphany to help propel you forward. This card encourages you to use your intelligence and mental prowess to embark on a new project. The road to victory will not be smooth or without struggle, so stay focused and clear-headed.

REVERSED KEY WORDS: Confusion, Lack of Clarity, Obstacles, Chaos

Reversed Meaning

Your judgement is clouded, and you are having trouble deciding the next move forward. You lack the clarity and necessary information to formulate a plan. The Ace of Swords reversed highlights confusion that you are feeling, and as a result, you may be experiencing some chaos. There are obstacles keeping you from advancing, so rethink your situation and try again once you have a clear focus.

Love and Relationships

When it comes to love, the Ace of Swords encourages you to remove toxic people or relationships from your life. Those seeking romance may find an intelligent partner to communicate with. Partnered couples facing challenges are encouraged to be clear and truthful about their needs to increase understanding.

Career and Wealth

You are facing a new beginning in your career that will allow you to make use of your intellect and mental gifts. The challenge is exciting, and like-minded colleagues will help you grow and learn. The Ace of Swords asks you to take a logical approach to your finances for security, instead of spending emotionally.

Success and Happiness

New ideas and ventures offer you the potential for success and happiness. The Ace of Swords represents the need for clarity and focus to achieve your goals. Use your insight and mental power to lead you to accomplishment, as this card symbolizes success in your endeavors.

Wild Card

This is a card of power, and at times you are asked to understand the responsibility that comes with it. You are in a position to influence a situation toward a positive outcome, so plan wisely and carefully. Honor your convictions and stand up for what is right.

TWO OF SWORDS

2 OF SWORDS

NUMEROLOGY: Choices

ASTROLOGY: Libra

ELEMENT: Air

COLORS: Blue, Gray, Yellow, Brown, White

SYMBOLS: Blindfold, Moon, Sea, Bench, White Robe, Rocks

Upright Meaning

The blindfold must come off, truth must be faced, and decisions must be made. The Two of Swords indicates you have a difficult decision to make and either will not accept the truth or are blind to it. You may not be fully aware of your circumstances, causing a stalemate. Both choices are equal in weight, and the best outcome is uncertain. This card asks you to weigh the pros and cons carefully and make an informed choice.

REVERSED KEY WORDS: Taking Action, Release, Making Choices, Moving Forward

Reversed Meaning

Your clarity has arrived, and you know what you need to do. Reversed, the Two of Swords finds you in a situation where you finally receive the information needed to make a hard decision. You are no longer stuck and are taking action to move forward. This card shows you releasing yourself from feeling trapped, and you are able to shift your position.

Love and Relationships

People interested in relationships are having difficulty making a decision, likely between potential partners. The Two of Swords also suggests there is a choice between choosing commitment or staying single. Those in relationships may be at a stalemate, and problems are not being resolved. Communication is suggested so you can move ahead.

Career and Wealth

You are facing a choice in your career, likely which path to pursue, that has you feeling stuck. Not all of the information is presented to you, making it difficult to decide the best option. This card suggests doing research before choosing. Financially, you may be avoiding choices in your budget.

Success and Happiness

To achieve peace or happiness, you must take action to uproot yourself from your current situation. Success is possible once you gain the clarity and resources needed to charge forward. The Two of Swords asks you to find balance and take action toward your dreams.

Wild Card

This card can be a reminder to face your problems head on rather than avoiding them. You are invited to make your choices in life with good intentions while being aware of all consequences. You are asked to take action and do what is necessary to move forward.

3 OF SWORDS

NUMEROLOGY: **Growth**

ASTROLOGY: **Libra**

ELEMENT: **Air**

COLORS: **Red, Silver, Gray**

SYMBOLS: **Clouds, Swords, Heart**

Upright Meaning

This is a card of deep sorrow and emotional pain. When the Three of Swords emerges in readings, you are experiencing heartbreak. Often, the sadness you are feeling is from an unexpected situation that has caught you off guard. This card reflects the need for emotional release, asking you to feel the grief and work through it. A good cry is suggested for coping and letting go of the pain. The hurt from the Three of Swords is always temporary.

REVERSED KEY WORDS: Release, Recovery, Mended Heart, Relief from Pain

Reversed Meaning

After a period of deep sorrow, the Three of Swords reversed signifies relief from the pain. There is a release from the suffering and grieving, as though a weight has been lifted. Your heart is healing, and you are recovering from the grief. At times, this card shows you struggling to move on from heartbreak. You have been unable to move forward and get past the pain. This card asks you to accept your circumstances to find peace.

Love and Relationships

Relationships are struggling when the Three of Cards is drawn in readings. There may be arguments, a rough patch, separation, or an ending of the relationship. This is a time of sorrow, heartbreak, and emotional pain, but there is a possibility of new things out there. Singles need to heal past trauma before seeking new love.

Career and Wealth

Your career is causing you grief and frustration. There may be a job loss ahead or a conflict with your coworkers. The Three of Swords advises an honest approach to working through the tension. Financial or material loss is possible right now, and your attention is needed to keep things afloat.

Success and Happiness

Reach out to others now for support so you can realign with a path to happiness. Success is still possible, but first you must release the past trauma that is holding you back. The pain is temporary, and as time passes, things will improve.

Wild Card

There are times when this card symbolizes words being taken to heart. You are absorbing the projections of others and allowing them to affect your emotional state. Find forgiveness and compassion for others to change the dynamic and adjust your perspective.

4 OF SWORDS

NUMEROLOGY: **Planning**

ASTROLOGY: **Libra**

ELEMENT: **Air**

COLORS: **Yellow, Gray, Red, Blue, Brown**

SYMBOLS: **Coffin, Stained Glass, Swords, Gray Walls**

Upright Meaning

You are on the brink of burning out after a long period of struggle. Exhaustion has you less productive and possibly stagnant, so the Four of Swords encourages you to rest. This card indicates a need to recuperate and recharge. Taking time away and focusing on yourself is advised. Meditate and take it easy, with a break from the overdrive. A period of contemplation is recommended before proceeding.

REVERSED KEY WORDS: Renewed Energy, Action, Healing, Recovery

Reversed Meaning

After a period of rest, the Four of Swords reversed symbolizes renewed energy. You are back in the action and well rested after some much-needed time away. The reversal of this card reveals recovery and healing after physical and mental overload. You are eager to get back to the action and start making things happen. Restlessness is possible, so be sure to avoid burnout by pacing yourself and not taking on too much at once.

Love and Relationships

It's time to take a break and rest with your partner, such as a vacation. On the other hand, the Four of Swords can indicate the need for a break from the relationship. You may need to put things on pause and reassess. If you are looking for love, be mindful not to exhaust yourself seeking a partner.

Career and Wealth

The stress from your career is catching up with you. You are overworked and exhausted. Time resting and recuperating is necessary with the Four of Swords. Take some time off to sleep and recharge to refresh your mental state. Financial stress has you overthinking your monetary situation, and a break from worrying will be helpful.

Success and Happiness

You need some time to yourself to meditate and contemplate your situation and where you would like to go with your vision. Have faith that success and happiness are possible with the Four of Swords. But you must rest and take time to regenerate yourself before pushing forward.

Wild Card

Solitude and the need to withdraw can be an aspect of the Four of Swords. You must spend some time alone and reconnect with yourself. This time is meant to be used to contemplate the progress you have made so far. Ground yourself and prepare to reignite your spark.

5 OF SWORDS

NUMEROLOGY: Conflict

ASTROLOGY: Aquarius

ELEMENT: Air

COLORS: Green, Red, Blue, Yellow, Gray

SYMBOLS: Water, Clouds, Swords

Upright Meaning

You are walking away from a situation with sadness and feelings of defeat. The conflict was so full of venom that negativity hangs over you and the situation. Even if you have not been defeated, the Five of Swords indicates that victory is spoiled by all that has been lost along the way. The aftermath is not worth having won the competition. This card reflects the importance of picking your battles wisely.

REVERSED KEY WORDS: Vindication, Moving Forward, Reconciliation

Reversed Meaning

After a time of disagreement, you have reached a point where you no longer want the conflict to continue. You are ready to reconcile and make peace. The Five of Swords reversed portrays moving forward from conflict instead of looking back or staying within the competition. Now it is time to rethink the way you approach situations. This reversal prompts you to take the high road more often instead of jumping into every fight.

Love and Relationships

There are arguments and conflict with your partner, causing tension in your relationship. You are feeling irritable and on edge. Sometimes you are arguing just for the sake of being right. The Five of Swords asks you to consider the cause of conflict in your relationship in order to work toward positive change.

Career and Wealth

There is hostility at work and poor communication among your colleagues. The misunderstandings are creating a negative environment that affects your career status. Money matters may be tight, and financial caution is recommended. Stay alert for others trying to take more than their share.

Success and Happiness

You have been battling through lately, and success may be delayed. For happiness to bloom, take stock of how you treat yourself. Self-sabotage may be holding you back from fully flourishing. The cost of winning may not be worth the battle, so take time to rethink your approach.

Wild Card

Sometimes this card is about apology. There is a need to make amends and smooth over any disagreements. Being right is not worth the conflict, and the Five of Swords suggests forgiveness and peace instead of constant fighting.

6 OF SWORDS

NUMEROLOGY: Harmony

ASTROLOGY: Aquarius

ELEMENT: Air

COLORS: Red, Black, Blue, Brown, Green

SYMBOLS: Shawl, Boat, Water, Oar, Tree

UPRIGHT KEY WORDS: Positive Transition, Brighter Days, Moving Forward, Travel, Releasing Baggage

Upright Meaning

This card finds you moving forward into new territory. Releasing the familiar is difficult but necessary, and the Six of Swords indicates that change is positive as you leave behind old baggage and welcomes new beginnings. Let go of what you no longer need in order to make way for transformation. The weight and trauma of the past must be left behind.

REVERSED KEY WORDS: Rough Times, Delays, No Progress, Stuck, Resistance

Reversed Meaning

Change is necessary, but you are avoiding it. You are reluctant to move forward and are expressing resistance to transition. The Six of Swords reversed portrays delays in your plans. You are not making progress and are approaching difficult times ahead. Unresolved conflict or trauma must be resolved so you can continue on your journey.

Love and Relationships

A situation that has been causing conflict in the relationship is coming to a close. You are moving on to better times together and leaving the past behind you. The Six of Swords portrays resolutions after disagreements. If you are seeking love, this card asks you to leave your past baggage behind you before committing to a relationship.

Career and Wealth

You are making progress and are headed toward positive outcomes. Improvement in your performance and overall career are shown by this card. Work stress is behind you as you sail into better times. Financial struggles are behind you as well, leaving you in a better place with money.

Success and Happiness

Your situation is improving, and success and happiness are in alignment. You are headed in the right direction. A more peaceful period is approaching as you transition into a more promising position. This card often speaks of being divinely guided on your journey to happiness.

Wild Card

Literal travel is possible with the Six of Swords. When this card appears in readings, you may be considering moving or visiting somewhere far from home. Your trip will be adventurous and freeing, helping you heal and move forward. This card offers personal growth and development.

SEVEN OF SWORDS

7 OF SWORDS

NUMEROLOGY: **Reflection**

ASTROLOGY: **Aquarius**

ELEMENT: **Air**

COLORS: **Yellow, Blue, Red, Green, Brown**

SYMBOLS: **Military Camp, City, Flag**

Upright Meaning

You are being deceptive and trying to go unnoticed in an effort to get away with something. The consequences of being caught are not ideal, and the weight of your actions will stay with you regardless. The Seven of Swords can also depict a time when someone is betraying you or cheating you. You may not be aware of the secrets behind your back. This card alerts you to the intentions behind the actions of others.

REVERSED KEY WORDS: Self-Deception, Feeling Fraudulent, Resisting Temptation

Reversed Meaning

Intense self-doubt has you feeling like a fraud. You don't feel qualified, capable, or worthy of your career or relationship. The Seven of Swords reversed shows your lack of self-worth holding you back from success. Self-deception has you convincing yourself that your inner voice is correct, instead of seeing the truth in situations. However, at times the reversal shows you resisting temptation and staying true to yourself and others.

Love and Relationships

In relationships, the Seven of Swords is an unwelcome card to draw. Someone is being dishonest or deceptive—either you or your partner. This card can indicate cheating, or on a less severe note, someone's feeling being spared. There is suspicion, and those seeking love are advised to proceed with caution.

Career and Wealth

Coworkers are behaving in an untrustworthy manner, and you are advised to watch out for trickery. Strategic planning is necessary on your end with the Seven of Swords. Protect your projects and your reputation. Your finances are at risk right now—watch for scams or theft of your money.

Success and Happiness

Follow your intuition as opposed to outside influences to achieve success and happiness. The Seven of Swords recommends that you develop a strategy to reach your goals. Rearrange your priorities to get you where you want to be in life, and leave behind what you can no longer carry.

Wild Card

Strategy is a significant message with the Seven of Swords. There are times when you need to prioritize what is important so you can get everything done. You may need to put yourself first at times and shift your responsibilities. Taking necessary shortcuts will resolve conflicts and accomplish goals right now.

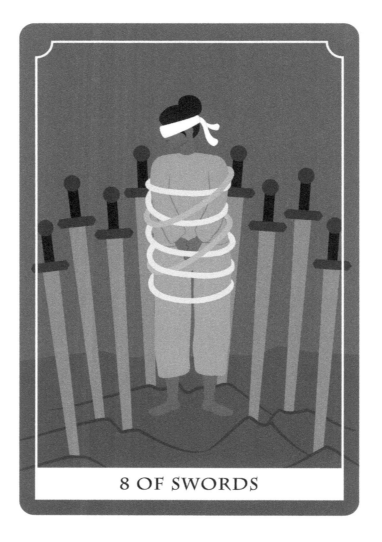

8 OF SWORDS

NUMEROLOGY: **Movement**

ASTROLOGY: **Gemini**

ELEMENT: **Air**

COLORS: **White, Red, Gray, Brown, Blue**

SYMBOLS: **Blindfold, Rope, Puddle**

UPRIGHT KEY WORDS: Victim Mindset, Feeling Trapped, Self-Imposed Limitations, Negativity, Helpless

Upright Meaning

Your circumstances have you feeling trapped and victimized. The Eight of Swords explains that this is not the case. Once you remove your blindfold, you realize your limits were self-imposed and things are not as bad as they seem. A simple step forward is all you need to gain control. Your thoughts may be negative and anxious with this card.

REVERSED KEY WORDS: Possibility, Empowerment, Clarity, Stepping Forward, Freeing Oneself, Releasing Negativity

Reversed Meaning

Possibility has presented itself to you. You no longer feel like a victim, trapped in self-imposed circumstances. Rather, you have taken a step forward and freed yourself. There is a release from negativity with the Eight of Swords reversed. You gain clarity and the power to take control of your circumstances. Any limiting beliefs about yourself no longer serve you.

Love and Relationships

Those seeking relationships may need to step outside the box and expand their search a bit further. To find a partner, you must take action with the Eight of Swords. Current relationships find a partner feeling trapped, smothered, or without choices, but communication reveals this is not the case.

Career and Wealth

You are feeling stuck in your career right now, with no other options or means. You have convinced yourself this is as good as it gets with work. Think outside the box and gather resources to shift your career. Finances are tight, and creative ideas can bring in more money.

Success and Happiness

The power to manifest success and happiness is within you when the Eight of Swords emerges. You may feel stuck or anxious when it comes to prosperity, but this card reveals you only need to take a step forward for change to begin.

Wild Card

Sometimes this card has you uncertain about which direction to go. Your anxiety and worry have you caught up in negative outcomes, so you stay in one place, unable to move in either direction. The Eight of Swords suggests connecting to your inner voice, trusting that you already know the best answer.

NINE OF SWORDS

9 OF SWORDS

NUMEROLOGY: **Attainment**

ASTROLOGY: **Gemini**

ELEMENT: **Air**

COLORS: **Black, White, Blue, Red, Yellow**

SYMBOLS: **Bed, Wall, Quilt, Roses**

Upright Meaning

Your worries and excessive anxiety are keeping you up at night. Fear is weighing you down, and the Nine of Swords shows that you are going through a dark mental process. Your worries seem much worse than they actually are, trapping you in this endless cycle of despair and mental torment. Understand how exaggerated your mind has made your troubles, and work on shifting your focus to free yourself from this anguish.

REVERSED KEY WORDS: Unfounded Worries, Good News, Relief from Anxiety, Recovery

Reversed Meaning

Deep anxiety and worry have been making your life difficult, and now you are at a shifting point. You have faced your worries only to find that they are unfounded and not nearly as serious as your mind imagined. Relief from anxiety is approaching when the Nine of Swords is reversed. You can expect good news and a release from the mental torment you have been experiencing. This is a time of recovery.

Love and Relationships

There is mistrust and anxiety in your relationship. Perhaps you are not trusting your partner or are feeling insecure. The Nine of Swords represents fears that may be unfounded, so reevaluate the source and work through these issues. Single people are asked to heal their regrets and remorse before committing to another.

Career and Wealth

Work is stressful and overwhelming, and the Nine of Swords invites you to manage your anxiety to avoid career burnout. Your finances may be tight right now, but your worry is disproportionate to the actual severity of the situation. Financial advisors may help you assess your money matters.

Success and Happiness

Balance is missing right now, and your worries are hindering progress toward your goals. For success and happiness, you must first gain control of your obsessive thoughts and anxiety. The Nine of Swords suggests you are losing sleep over fears and need support to get back on track.

Wild Card

The only way out is through, and you are being asked to call on others for help. This card invites you to break the cycle of anxiety and examine your fears. The pattern of worry is affecting you negatively, and the Nine of Swords recommends seeking support to heal and move forward.

10 OF SWORDS

NUMEROLOGY: Transformation

ASTROLOGY: Gemini

ELEMENT: Air

COLORS: Black, Brown, Red, Yellow, Blue

SYMBOLS: Cape, Water, Mountains

UPRIGHT KEY WORDS: Difficult Endings, Painful Situation, Rock Bottom, Betrayal, Ending a Cycle

Upright Meaning

You have reached rock bottom and are experiencing what feels like a very painful ending to a situation. While the end is inevitable, it is often unexpected and accompanied by feelings of betrayal. The Ten of Swords marks the ending of a difficult cycle, and with this comes the knowledge that things can only get better from here. Getting through the pain may not be easy, but gain hope knowing that you are facing the worst of it.

REVERSED KEY WORDS: End of Suffering, Relief, Better Times, Improvement, Recovery, Resistance

Reversed Meaning

The end of suffering is approaching, and you are about to feel much-needed relief from a painful situation. Reversed, better times are around the corner, and you can expect improvement in your life. This is a period of recovery and healing. At times, this reversal can reveal you are resisting inevitable change and must find acceptance.

Love and Relationships

Relationships are facing a possible ending or a difficult time ahead. There are feelings of sadness and grief, as well as the likelihood of betrayal. The Ten of Swords offers acceptance. Those seeking partnership must first heal old wounds before entering a committed relationship.

Career and Wealth

You are reaching the end of a cycle in your career. Likely your job position is coming to a close or you are changing to a new area. This card finds you feeling overwhelmed, and possibly betrayed by coworkers. You are experiencing a loss financially, and money matters are looking bleak.

Success and Happiness

Success and happiness will come once you let go of what may be holding you back and cut ties with anything weighing you down. If you have hit a wall, the Ten of Swords asks you to accept where you are and reformulate your plan.

Wild Card

You are being asked to accept your situation and avoid playing the victim for sympathy. The Ten of Swords can reveal that you are struggling to let go with grace and instead are seeking pity or prolonging the inevitable. This card encourages reflection and acceptance.

PAGE OF SWORDS

NUMEROLOGY: Formation

ASTROLOGY: Libra

ELEMENT: Air

COLORS: Blue, Green, Yellow, Purple, Red

SYMBOLS: Mountains, Uneven Ground, Breeze

UPRIGHT KEY WORDS: Curiosity, New Ideas, Innovative Communication, Wanting to Learn, Decisive

Upright Meaning

Excitement about new possibilities and ideas flows through the Page of Swords. When this card emerges, you are full of curiosity and eager to explore new methods. You are shifting your thoughts and trying to learn as much as possible. This is a "yes" card for moving forward with your new ideas. You are encouraged to try different techniques until you find the best direction to follow your passion.

REVERSED KEY WORDS: Inaction, No Results, Disorganization, Hindered Expression

Reversed Meaning

There is much to say, but you are holding back from speaking your truth. Fear has you keeping your thoughts to yourself rather than of sharing your voice. The Page of Swords reversed wants you to speak up and bring your private thoughts to the public. Your message is worth sharing. This card can show a lack of action and projects that never take off.

Love and Relationships

Your relationship is one of intellect and deep conversations. Emotionally, there may be some resistance or lack of affection. The Page of Swords in love readings suggests communicating your emotional needs and ensuring there is enough intimacy. Those seeking love will gain by socializing more and staying patient when it comes to meeting someone.

Career and Wealth

Your intelligence is opening doors and placing you ahead in your career. New ideas are being considered, and you are encouraged to learn more about your craft to further your skill set. Think of creative ways to increase your money and secure your finances.

Success and Happiness

There is opportunity here for success and happiness. To ensure you are on the right track, feed your curiosity. Keep learning and interacting with others to bring in what you are seeking. The Page of Swords shows your charisma helping you get ahead.

Wild Card

Adjust your communication with others when the Page of Swords comes along. The way you are interacting isn't working, so think outside the box and change your methods. Sharing and expression is important, so work to find an easier way.

KNIGHT OF SWORDS

KNIGHT OF SWORDS

NUMEROLOGY: **Growth**

ASTROLOGY: **Libra**

ELEMENT: **Air**

COLORS: **Blue, Yellow, Red, Gray, White**

SYMBOLS: **Horse, Clouds, Armor, Feathers**

Upright Meaning

You are a highly ambitious and motivated person, full of determination when it comes to following your dreams. When you are on a mission, nothing gets in your way. The Knight of Swords does not plan ahead but rather is driven by the energy and excitement of action. You are quick-witted and intelligent, as well as courageous. This card shows you have a successful mindset and are full of determination.

REVERSED KEY WORDS: Reckless Behavior, Aggression, Rash Actions, Restless, No Focus

Reversed Meaning

All of your ideas and energy are bottled up and stuck inside when the Knight of Swords is reversed. You are restless and feeling blocked from taking action. Finding focus is difficult for you, and you may be acting rashly out of frustration. There are times when this card reversed shows aggression or reckless behavior. You are acting out without putting any thought into the consequences. Focus and slow your mind.

Love and Relationships

Those seeking love must take action to find a partner with the Knight of Swords. Be courageous and bold to bring in new love. Relationships may be struggling with lack of commitment or a bored partner. The lack of intimacy and emotional bonding is becoming an issue.

Career and Wealth

You are efficient and ambitious. You are tackling work projects head on, and your fearless approach is opening doors and offering progress. Moving up is likely with the Knight of Swords. Monetary goals are being reached thanks to your financial focus. For security, keep saving and stay determined.

Success and Happiness

Change is in the air, and everything is starting to come together. The Knight of Swords asks you to jump at the opportunities being presented to you for success and happiness. Things are looking up for prosperity, and good news is likely. Stay driven and courageous on your path.

Wild Card

Your intellect is a favorable attribute, and worldly discussions and connections excite you. Speaking on all matters comes easily to you, and you seek out other like-minded people to engage with. This card cautions against acting without thinking things through, as the Knight of Swords tends to do.

QUEEN OF SWORDS

QUEEN OF SWORDS

NUMEROLOGY: Stability

ASTROLOGY: Libra

ELEMENT: Air

COLORS: Blue, Gray, White, Yellow, Red

SYMBOLS: Crown, Butterflies, Clouds, Throne

UPRIGHT KEY WORDS: Independence, Intellect, Fairness, Direct Approach, Boundaries

Upright Meaning

The Queen of Swords is fiercely independent and capable. It shows you are very intelligent, with mental clarity and the ability to assess a situation. Fairness and discernment aid you as you seek the truth. With this card, you deliver your message without hesitation or distraction. You communicate directly and honestly, leaving no room for uncertainty. You lead from the head, without emotional influence.

REVERSED KEY WORDS: Cold, Mean, Sentimental, Impressionable, Involvement

Reversed Meaning

Your direct manner has turned into a cold approach. Interactions with you are unpleasant, as you can be mean and cruel. The Queen of Swords reversed has taken fairness to an extreme. Other times, this reversal indicates you have become overly emotional and sentimental. There is a lack of control making you easy to influence. Others may manipulate you when the Queen is reversed, so be mindful of their intentions.

Love and Relationships

Single people may be enjoying their space and independence, so relationships are not necessarily a priority. Those in relationships may be experiencing a need for boundaries. Partners with the Queen of Swords are loyal but not quick to show romance.

Career and Wealth

There is a mentor at your workplace offering you valuable advice. Alternatively, the Queen of Swords shows you excelling in your career due to your intellect and direct communication skills. You are respected by your peers. Financially, boundaries and balance are needed when it comes to lending your money to others.

Success and Happiness

Your wisdom and intellect are guiding you toward prosperity with the Queen of Swords. Success and happiness can be found with this card, which invites you to draw on your past experiences for insight and guidance.

Wild Card

Boundaries are significant with the Queen of Swords. You are encouraged to establish clear boundaries and stick to them with people, situations, and behaviors that affect you negatively. Sticking to this expectation sets a clear precedent and helps you navigate through life with more strength and directness.

KING OF SWORDS

NUMEROLOGY: **Change**

ASTROLOGY: **Libra**

ELEMENT: **Air**

COLORS: **Blue, Purple, Red, Yellow, Gray**

SYMBOLS: **Throne, Crown, Butterflies, Moon, Clouds, Robe, Cloak**

Upright Meaning

Authority is respected when you are in command with the King of Swords. Your intelligence and courage put you in a place of power, and others recognize your position with interest. You are a wise leader who is fair and rational in your actions. This card finds you seeking the truth in situations, and you command others without bias. Mental clarity aids you in your decisions as you continue with your accomplishments.

REVERSED KEY WORDS: Self-Serving, Delayed Decisions, Lacking Fairness, Manipulation, Abuse of Power

Reversed Meaning

Power is being misused when the King of Swords is reversed. Your intelligence and authority have gone to your head, and you now act with selfishness. You are manipulating others to your advantage and not coming from a place of fairness. The reversal shows you delaying action on matters and using others for self-gain. You are advised to go within and reflect on your behavior.

Love and Relationships

Romantic relationships are built on respect and logic with the King of Swords. There is a lack of emotional outpouring, as your partner leans toward intellect over sentiment. Together you encourage each other toward goals. Singles may have high standards that make finding a partner challenging.

Career and Wealth

Your high standards help your career. Challenge yourself and stick to your personal principles. The King of Swords can represent a mentor who leads you. Financially, discipline and logic are needed to get ahead. Large purchases need thought before proceeding.

Success and Happiness

Structure and routine will help you toward success and happiness. Gather all of the knowledge and experience you have acquired, and put it into motion. Your commanding authority will support your progress. Be mindful to allow some emotional expression along the way.

Wild Card

The King of Swords can represent a literal person at times, particularly one in a professional role like law or finance. If you have called on someone for help, they are qualified and experienced to help advise you in your circumstances.

CHAPTER 10

THE MINOR ARCANA: WANDS

THIS CHAPTER COVERS THE MINOR ARCANA suit of Wands, explaining what these cards represent in tarot readings. Wands portray energy, inspirations, ideas, and creativity. Wands speak of determination, spirituality, ambition, and other aspects of motivation and creation. Passion, expansion, and drive are common elements of Wands. This is a suit of inspired action. This chapter explains the key words and meanings for each card in the suit, from the Ace (which is one) through the King of Wands.

ACE OF WANDS

ACE OF WANDS

NUMEROLOGY: Opportunity

ASTROLOGY: Aries

ELEMENT: Fire

COLORS: Green, Purple, Yellow, Blue, White

SYMBOLS: Landscape, Mountains, River, Sky, Hand, Cloud, Leaves, Castle

Upright Meaning

Follow your passion when the Ace of Wands appears. This card expresses potential and new opportunities for you. The ideas that inspire you are very energetic in nature, full of creativity and spirit. You are motivated and ready to follow your heart. When you are on the fence about starting a new venture, this card is a nod to follow your passion. You must take action and put in the work to see a satisfying end result.

REVERSED KEY WORDS: Delays, False Starts, Setbacks, Hesitation, No Direction

Reversed Meaning

Unformulated ideas are circling your head, but you are not sure in which direction to go. There are inspirations you would like to explore, but you lack direction to bring projects to fruition. With the Ace of Wands reversed, you are experiencing delays and setbacks in your ventures. You may have started only to find you were not actually ready or prepared. The hesitation you are feeling prompts you to be patient and redirect your passion.

Love and Relationships

If you are seeking love, the Ace of Wands signifies a very passionate, exciting new partnership approaching. Couples are encouraged to become flirtatious and rekindle their romance. Display your attraction to each other. This card invites you to connect more deeply on an emotional level.

Career and Wealth

Financial hardships are beginning to turn around when the Ace of Wands is drawn. A bonus or monetary increase may be given. Your career is expanding, with new opportunities opening up. You are feeling inspired and are encouraged to put your creative energy to good use in your work.

Success and Happiness

This is a card that speaks of good news for success and happiness. There are new opportunities for you to act on, and they are encouraging with the Ace of Wands. Your inspiration and ideas are likely to be prosperous if you put in the effort and stay committed.

Wild Card

Self-improvement and personal growth are attributes that can appear with the Ace of Wands. Connecting spiritually or expanding your creative side are encouraged with this card. The opportunity to learn and try new things presents itself, allowing you to branch out even further. Take this chance to delve deeper into yourself.

TWO OF WANDS

2 OF WANDS

NUMEROLOGY: Choices

ASTROLOGY: Aries

ELEMENT: Fire

COLORS: Brown, Orange, Red, White, Purple

SYMBOLS: Globe, Castle Wall, Town, Land, Sea, Mountains

UPRIGHT KEY WORDS: Progress, Planning, Choices, Exploring

Upright Meaning

The Two of Wands indicates you are in a planning stage. Your inspirations have you motivated, and now you are working out the details. You have made progress in your endeavors and have the dedication to follow through. This card finds you making changes that place you outside of your comfort zone so you can bring your dreams to life.

REVERSED KEY WORDS: Inactivity, Wrong Direction, Untapped Potential

Reversed Meaning

Your ideas are stagnating. The Two of Wands reversed finds you lacking action when it comes to your inspiration. You have untapped potential. Branching out into new realms has you reluctant, causing delayed ventures. You may have started following through on your plans only to realize you veered off in the wrong direction. This card asks you to find your spark so you can start putting your plans into motion.

Love and Relationships

It may be time to take your relationship to the next level of commitment. Put your plans into action together to ensure a positive outcome long-term. The Two of Wands shows that those looking for romance will find potential suitors and start new relationships.

Career and Wealth

You are making plans and putting together the details to follow your inspiration in your career. Shifting focus or venturing out on your own is likely with the Two of Wands. Financially, you are comfortable and stable.

Success and Happiness

Explore your options to put yourself on the best path to success and happiness. Your future looks promising, and the outlook is encouraging. Look ahead and take action to manifest your dreams, as your talent is recognized. Put careful detail into your plan to ensure success.

Wild Card

There is a choice that needs to be made, and the unknown has you reluctant to step forward. You are deciding between the familiar and the new, with the Two of Wands prompting you to be bold and discover more for yourself. Move beyond what you know and into new territory.

THREE OF WANDS

3 OF WANDS

NUMEROLOGY: Expansion

ASTROLOGY: Leo

ELEMENT: Fire

COLORS: Yellow, Red, Black, White, Green

SYMBOLS: Ship, Sea, Mountains, Land

Upright Meaning

You are making considerable progress toward your goals, and the Three of Wands recognizes your steady pace and strong planning. More opportunities are possible when this card appears, and you are being asked to broaden your horizons. Expansion will further your advancement and help you progress. You are doing well with planning for the long term and are committed to your vision. Obstacles are recognized in advance as you navigate with confidence.

REVERSED KEY WORDS: Unaccomplished, Lack of Planning, Delays, Small Steps

Reversed Meaning

You are ignoring the leaps and strides needed to accomplish your dreams. Instead, you are taking small steps and playing it safe. Stepping outside the box is necessary, yet you are limiting opportunity by staying in your comfort zone. Reversed, the Three of Wands shows improper planning on your part that can lead to delays and unexpected setbacks. You are not achieving your goals or fulfilling your inspirations when this card is reversed.

Love and Relationships

People looking for relationships are encouraged to travel or expand their social settings to meet their future partner. New places offer potential for love. Those already paired have created a solid foundation and are very committed. The Three of Wands shows romance and a steady progression in your relationship.

Career and Wealth

Your career can benefit from expansion or stepping outside your comfort zone. There are opportunities to jump on, and the Three of Wands invites confidence and adventurous choices. Financially, you are able to enjoy the results of your hard work and spend some money on new experiences or travel arrangements.

Success and Happiness

The progress you are making is paving the way to success and happiness with the Three of Wands. You are planning and working hard to advance further. This card indicates adventure and feeling free, prompting you to stay confident and continue forward.

Wild Card

There are instances when the Three of Wands refers to literal travel. This travel is often far away or overseas or related to the water. You may be offered a job opportunity that involves relocating. This card speaks of adventure and discovering new areas.

FOUR OF WANDS

4 OF WANDS

NUMEROLOGY: **Foundation**

ASTROLOGY: **Sagittarius**

ELEMENT: **Fire**

COLORS: **Yellow, Orange, Red, Green, Blue**

SYMBOLS: **Chuppah, Roses, Grapes, Castle, Flower Bouquet**

Upright Meaning

A welcome card in tarot readings, the Four of Wands symbolizes celebration. Milestones are achieved, and it is time to rejoice with loved ones. This card often revolves around home and reuniting with family. A solid foundation has been established in your life, and now you are unwinding and enjoying the fruits of your labor. You are feeling harmony and joy. This is a period of relaxation after major shifting and growing, with peace and happiness.

REVERSED KEY WORDS: Delayed Celebration, Inner Harmony, Impending Success, Conflict

Reversed Meaning

Reversed, the Four of Wands holds similar meaning to the upright position. There is reason to celebrate, but there may be a delay in the celebration. Success is on the way, but it just hasn't arrived yet. Reversed, this card reveals that the joy you are experiencing is internal, based on personal or private victories. The reversal can also indicate conflict and tension between loved ones and feelings of instability. Upheaval during life changes is possible.

Love and Relationships

People looking for relationships are encouraged to expand their search through family events and celebrations. Community settings are suggested for finding a partner with the Four of Wands. Couples have a strong foundation and are becoming closer and reaching a milestone such as engagement or marriage.

Career and Wealth

Your work environment is very social and united among your peers. Stability is found in your career, and you may have a reason to celebrate soon. The Four of Wands shows a happy workplace. Finances are secure, and you enjoy treating loved ones to gifts and outings.

Success and Happiness

A good sign for success and happiness comes with the Four of Wands. You have built a solid ground to work from and are near a point of celebration. Loved ones support you and encourage you as you move forward. Harmony and a period of relaxation are on the way.

Wild Card

When this card appears, marriage is a likely possibility. The Four of Wands represents unity and coming together and can refer to engagements or marriage. There is a milestone or reason to celebrate with this card, and relationships are often referenced. The Four of Wands presents a reason to dance and feel joyful.

5 OF WANDS

NUMEROLOGY: Conflict

ASTROLOGY: Leo

ELEMENT: Fire

COLORS: Red, Blue, White, Green, Yellow

SYMBOLS: Wands, Clothing

Upright Meaning

Competition is delaying your progress, and you are dealing with conflict in a situation. Those around you have differing thoughts with everyone listening to themselves but no one else. There is an element of jealousy and disagreement with the Five of Wands. This card shows diversity and invites you to come together to create change and find resolution.

REVERSED KEY WORDS: Peace, Resolved Conflict, Focused Energy, Release, Avoiding Conflict, Inner Turmoil

Reversed Meaning

When this card is reversed, you are facing conflict and turmoil, but this time it is internal. Your thoughts are holding you back, and you are comparing yourself to others and perhaps feeling a bit jealous. Other times, the Five of Wands reversed finds you avoiding conflict and trying to keep the peace. You are focusing and channeling your energy for the better. This card shows a peaceful resolution or a resolved conflict. There is a release from the tension.

Love and Relationships

Single people are finding several suitors interested in them at the same time. There is competition among potential partners, and you must decide whom to engage with. The Five of Wands reveals couples face increased tension and should focus on lightening the mood.

Career and Wealth

Your career is full of competition and conflict. The nature of your work is tense, and you are at odds with others. The Five of Wands signifies you have what it takes to overcome this challenge. Money matters are imbalanced, and there is a need to regain financial stability.

Success and Happiness

Your competitive streak can help you get ahead, but first you must find inner peace and tame the conflict in your mind once you resolve the tension. The Five of Wands suggests first becoming more organized and structured.

Wild Card

Transformation is inevitable, and this card can reveal that you are resisting change. The Five of Wands prompts you to rein in your chaotic energy and face your challenges with excitement instead of trepidation. Find more purpose to help you progress with clarity.

6 OF WANDS

NUMEROLOGY: **Harmony**

ASTROLOGY: **Aries**

ELEMENT: **Fire**

COLORS: **Green, Red, Yellow, Blue**

SYMBOLS: **Crown, Laurel Wreath, Horse**

Upright Meaning

Another welcome card in tarot readings, the Six of Wands symbolizes success and victory. You have been working hard toward your dreams, and now you are being recognized for your accomplishments. This card finds you receiving public accolades for your goals, reminding you how far you have come. Triumph over obstacles is attained, and you are encouraged to be proud of your success. You have been given a boost of positive energy to keep going.

REVERSED KEY WORDS: Personal Accomplishments, Egotistical, Self-Doubt, Delayed Success

Reversed Meaning

Success has been achieved, but you prefer to keep the good news to yourself. Your personal accomplishments are being celebrated privately, as you are not comfortable sharing. The Six of Wands reversed finds you lacking confidence and feeling doubtful about your success. Other times, the reversal indicates that success has yet to arrive or goals have yet to be met. You may be acting egotistical and bitter that no one has congratulated your efforts.

Love and Relationships

People looking for love are likely to be successful with the Six of Wands. Your approach is attracting others, and they are open to connecting with you. Relationships have a happy future, and goals that you have been working toward are coming together nicely. There are feelings of joy and satisfaction.

Career and Wealth

Financially, you are in a good and stable place. Money matters are not a point of stress, and you can spend a bit indulgently now. The Six of Wands shows positive accomplishments in your career, and you are being recognized for your efforts. A promotion or bonus is possible.

Success and Happiness

Triumph and victory are approaching from the effort you have been putting into your goals. Success and happiness can be found with the Six of Wands, along with acclaim from others for your achievement. This card finds you at an advantage and that much closer to manifesting your dreams.

Wild Card

You are reminded that your latest accomplishment, although successful, is not the end of the finish line. Your hard work is showing, but you still have a ways to go before fully celebrating. The Six of Wands signifies there can still be challenges as you progress. Stay the course.

SEVEN OF WANDS

7 OF WANDS

NUMEROLOGY: Reflection

ASTROLOGY: Leo

ELEMENT: Fire

COLORS: Blue, Green, Yellow, Brown, White

SYMBOL: Wands

Upright Meaning

You are scrambling to get yourself together and fight sudden conflicts head on. The Seven of Wands portrays you surrounded by chaotic energy. Competition has you doing whatever it takes to protect yourself and your endeavors. This card represents your perseverance during adversity and shows you standing your ground. Be prepared to stay firm with your beliefs and not be swayed.

REVERSED KEY WORDS: Avoiding Conflict, Feeling Vulnerable, Intimidated, Overwhelmed, Burned Out

Reversed Meaning

In an attempt to avoid conflict, you avoid speaking the truth to others. The Seven of Wands reversed shows that you feel vulnerable and not protected. You are easily intimidated, but you must stand your ground.

Love and Relationships

Outside influences, such as family, work, or other suitors, are threatening your relationship, but you must stand your ground. Strong boundaries and firm resolution are needed. The Seven of Wands reminds those looking for love to keep persevering until it arrives.

Career and Wealth

Confidence is important to overcome the challenges you are facing in your career. Your position may be in question, and the Seven of Wands prompts you to remain fearless. Keep going and stand firm. Financially, long-term success is likely if you keep investing and stay diligent in money matters.

Success and Happiness

Stand your ground and stand up for yourself to see success and happiness. Fulfillment of your goals comes after some challenging situations with the Seven of Wands. You have what it takes to overcome these obstacles, so believe in yourself and stay persistent. This card reminds you of your strength.

Wild Card

Someone or something is trying to block the fulfillment of your project. There are times when the Seven of Wands indicates a competitive person or situation threatening the outcome of your endeavors. Create boundaries, and be aware of any possible obstacles.

EIGHT OF WANDS

8 OF WANDS

NUMEROLOGY: Movement

ASTROLOGY: Sagittarius

ELEMENT: Fire

COLORS: Brown, Green, Blue

SYMBOLS: Wands, Sprouting Leaves, Water

Movement, Quick Change, Sudden Shifts, Action, Falling into Place

Upright Meaning

You have momentum toward your goals, and positive change is around the corner. The Eight of Wands brings forth sudden shifts and quick changes. Suddenly, everything starts coming together and falling into place. This is a card of alignment and action. Focus on what you would like to bring in for yourself, and don't resist the transition. Go with the flow of this highly energetic card.

REVERSED KEY WORDS: Resisting Change, Delayed Outcomes, Feeling Frustrated, Lack of Focus

Reversed Meaning

Change is at your door, but you are fighting it. Sudden shifts leave you trying to control the outcome, but the Eight of Wands reversed advises against this fight. You may be experiencing delays and losing momentum. Frustration has you scattered, and your lack of focus is hindering your progress. This reversal recommends you reevaluate your plan of action.

Love and Relationships

Expect quick change if you are looking for romance with the Eight of Wands. Singles are encouraged to go with the flow and prepare to meet someone new soon. Relationships will see some happy surprises or positive changes. Romance and excitement are likely to increase with this card.

Career and Wealth

Swift movement forward will bring you to new heights in your career. Rapid changes are positive, and you are advancing with confidence with the Eight of Wands. Financially, your money comes in and out quickly, so watch your spending right now.

Success and Happiness

There is momentum and progress forward with the Eight of Wands. Positive change is coming, and the shifts are rapid. The Eight of Wands implores you to take action for success and happiness. Everything will come together and align for your greatest good.

Wild Card

In order to get what you want, you must act fast. Quick responses are crucial with the Eight of Wands, as you do not want to miss your window of opportunity. Take advantage of this high energy. At times, this card means air travel to faraway locations.

NINE OF WANDS

9 OF WANDS

NUMEROLOGY: **Attainment**

ASTROLOGY: **Sagittarius**

ELEMENT: **Fire**

COLORS: **Green, Brown, Gray, White**

SYMBOLS: **Bandage, Staff**

UPRIGHT KEY WORDS: Great Strength, Test of Faith, Resilience, Boundaries, Persistence, Bravery

Upright Meaning

In times of challenge, you still persist. The end of a struggle is almost near, and you have been through the battle. The Nine of Wands shows you have great strength and determination. You keep going even when you are down, putting on a brave face for the world. This feels like a test of faith, and you are still resilient through it all. This card encourages you to stay persistent and strong while jumping this final hurdle.

REVERSED KEY WORDS: Weakness, Avoiding Battle, Struggle, Unprepared

Reversed Meaning

You are not standing up for yourself when the Nine of Wands is reversed. You are feeling overwhelmed and choose to avoid battles and conflict. You are feeling weak, and your defenses are down. You are not prepared for the situation at hand and have been caught off guard. This reversal reminds you not to give up and to reach out to others for support.

Love and Relationships

Inner work and preparation are encouraged for people seeking partnership with the Nine of Wands. Stay persistent and keep going; your resilience will pay off. Relationships benefit from hard work and sacrifice at this time. Communication and adapting to each other's needs are attributes of this card.

Career and Wealth

Work has you exhausted, and the battle is almost finished. You have been putting in extra time and effort with the Nine of Wands, and you are exhibiting strength in your endeavors. Money matters can be tight, and this card prompts you to seek additional sources of income.

Success and Happiness

Push forward and stay strong in your quest for success and happiness. The Nine of Wands finds you close to your goals, but the road is not easy. It feels like a test of faith, and you are asked to persevere. The tide is starting to turn in your favor.

Wild Card

Boundaries need to be enforced with the Nine of Wands. Your energy needs protecting and conserving, so now is the time to get assertive. State your needs, put up walls, and draw lines. Allow support to help you get back on track while remaining aware of where you direct your energy.

TEN OF WANDS

10 OF WANDS

NUMEROLOGY: **Completion**

ASTROLOGY: **Leo**

ELEMENT: **Fire**

COLORS: **Brown, Green, Red, Blue, Orange**

SYMBOLS: **Sticks, Field, Town, Tree**

Upright Meaning

There is an added weight on your shoulders, as you are burdened by all of the work and responsibility that you have been undertaking. The Ten of Wands knows that you are close to accomplishing your goal, and here you are picking up the extra slack to get there. Feelings of being overwhelmed can benefit from time management and reprioritization when this card appears. You are encouraged to drop the weight and not carry it all on your own.

Reversed Meaning

After a period of taking on too much and going it alone, you have decided to start delegating your load to other people. You are simplifying your life and lessening your burdens. The Ten of Wands reversed depicts you releasing yourself from so much responsibility and relieving yourself from all that pressure. This reversal allows you to let go of what you have been bottling up inside, giving yourself a new sense of freedom.

Love and Relationships

Your relationship may be feeling burdened by responsibility. Romance has been pushed aside due to life stressors, and the Ten of Wands reminds you to ask your lover for help. Those seeking relationships are encouraged to spend some time alone practicing self-care before rushing in to care for a partner.

Career and Wealth

You are spread too thin at work and taking on too many projects. You are overworked and overwhelmed, and the Ten of Wands reminds you to delegate at work to ease your stress. Your finances are a bit of a burden right now, and your money is going to several different places at once.

Success and Happiness

Your end goal is in sight, and the Ten of Wands indicates a successful outcome. To achieve this happiness, you must unburden yourself of what weighs you down. Seek support from others and don't lose sight of your focus. You are headed in the right direction.

Wild Card

Goals have been met and accomplishments achieved, yet you still feel overwhelmed. There is a feeling of surprise that you still have so much responsibility. The Ten of Wands suggests transferring some tasks and responsibilities to others. Keep your inspirational spark.

PAGE OF WANDS

PAGE OF WANDS

NUMEROLOGY: **Choices**

ASTROLOGY: **Aries**

ELEMENT: **Fire**

COLORS: **Yellow, Black, Gray, Brown, Red**

SYMBOLS: **Hat, Feather, Cape, Pyramid, Salamander**

Upright Meaning

Endless possibilities excite you, and there are no limits to the many ideas running through your mind. There are sparks of inspiration, and you are eager to start exploring these opportunities. The Page of Wands has no real plans or strategy. Enthusiasm is enough for now. You are a free spirit, but a strategy or plan is helpful before you take off for adventure.

REVERSED KEY WORDS: Hesitant, Cautious, Erroneous Beliefs, Channeled Energy

Reversed Meaning

You have some vague ideas or are in the early stages of new potential, but you are not sure how to put it all together. This lack of direction has you cautious about moving forward. The Page of Wands reversed helps you figure out ways to channel your energy and ideas into something tangible. You may be doubting your abilities or hindering progress because of false beliefs about your capabilities.

Love and Relationships

There are new and different people to meet when the Page of Wands emerges. Those looking for a relationship are faced with different choices and exciting possibilities. Boredom is not an option. Couples are feeling adventurous and trying new experiences together. This card speaks of a lively and fun romance.

Career and Wealth

Unexpected monetary gifts or forms of income may suddenly appear with the Page of Wands. Your finances could use some extra padding and saving. New doors are opening in your career and taking a chance with your ideas is encouraged. Successful outcomes are likely.

Success and Happiness

Good news is approaching, and your free-spirited nature is excited by the possibilities. Your success and happiness are attainable with the Page of Wands. Before you rush forward without hesitation, this card reminds you that a plan can help you achieve your dreams with less chance of a setback.

Wild Card

Sometimes the Page of Wands symbolizes your spiritual path in life. Your curiosity may have led you to the beginning stages of a spiritual journey to connect to yourself on a deeper level. This card invites you to learn different elements of spirituality and seek someone to guide you through this adventure.

KNIGHT OF WANDS

KNIGHT OF WANDS

NUMEROLOGY: Growth

ASTROLOGY: Leo

ELEMENT: Fire

COLORS: Yellow, Black, Orange, Red, Blue

SYMBOLS: Desert, Plume, Tabard, Salamander, Horse, Armor

Upright Meaning

The Knight of Wands pursues goals with energy and high motivation. This card is full of inspiration and the actions taken to bring dreams to fruition. You are passionate and have an adventurous streak. At times, you can be impulsive in your actions. The Knight of Wands reveals you to be bold and courageous, and nothing can stop you from chasing your dreams. You embody charisma and high energy. This is a green light to proceed with plans.

REVERSED KEY WORDS: Overly Confident, Interruptions, Delays, Frustration

Reversed Meaning

You are bursting with energy and ideas, but they are stuck inside you. Unsure how to channel this energy, you have become frustrated and restless. The Knight of Wands reversed shows your plans are delayed in coming to fruition. Interruptions are hindering your progress. At times, this reversal finds you overly confident and impulsive to the point of detriment. You may be acting smug or presumptuous.

Love and Relationships

Your relationship is exciting but unstable, with adventure and risk coming before commitment and loyalty. The Knight of Wands shows an energetic and passionate partnership. Singles may meet a courageous and charming partner with impulsive ways in the near future. This card implies your suitor will be quite taken with you.

Career and Wealth

New projects and opportunities are enticing you in your career. You are full of enthusiasm and excitement, but the ventures are taking longer than expected. The Knight of Wands may find you frustrated until you increase your efforts. Finances are ample, and now is a good time to splurge.

Success and Happiness

Your ventures are likely to be even more successful than you imagined with the Knight of Wands. Energetic enthusiasm and confidence aid you in your progress, and happiness is near. Be careful not to rush in without a plan or a clear vision to ensure smooth sailing.

Wild Card

Your impulsive tendencies create situations where you act quickly without thinking about the consequences. Your energetic impatience causes delays and setbacks to your plans. The Knight of Wands invites you to strategize and think before acting.

QUEEN OF WANDS

QUEEN OF WANDS

NUMEROLOGY: Stability

ASTROLOGY: Aries

ELEMENT: Fire

COLORS: Yellow, Orange, Red, Black, Gray

SYMBOLS: Lion, Sunflower, Black Cat, Robe, Cloak, Crown

Upright Meaning

Courage and determination are well-known attributes of the Queen of Wands. The Queen is self-aware and full of inspired energy. You exude confidence and are not afraid to charge forward and follow your dreams. Driven by passion, you fight through obstacles and stay positive. A natural leader, you have a powerful influence. Socially, people flock to you and listen to your guidance. Your schedule is full of social events.

REVERSED KEY WORDS: Impatient, Without Limits, Temperamental, Introverted

Reversed Meaning

A lack of confidence has you withdrawn. You have lost your courage and your bold, energetic drive. Social scenes do not appeal to you, and attention from others is not preferred. The Queen of Wands reversed finds you feeling introverted and shut in. You may also feel full of impatience, to the point of temperamental behavior. Boundaries and limits are disregarded, and you plow through situations recklessly. This reversal can indicate an egotistical outlook.

Love and Relationships

Relationships are benefitting from a period of openness and honest communication with the Queen of Wands. Singles are encouraged not to worry how others view them and instead embrace their individuality when seeking a partner.

Career and Wealth

Your career is progressing due to your drive and high energy. Your projects and opportunities have the potential for success. The Queen of Wands shows you leading others. Your finances are in a good place, and you are able to expand your income with focus and smart decisions.

Success and Happiness

Your energy, passion, and drive are moving you forward to success and happiness. Confidence keeps you going past any challenges. This card is a good sign for continued prosperity. Stay mindful of which direction you are headed, as your high enthusiasm can lead you off course.

Wild Card

There are times when the Queen of Wands reveals the need to confront parts of yourself that may be unflattering or hidden. There are aspects of you that remain in the dark, and this card encourages you to bring them to the light. The Queen invites you to embrace yourself fully.

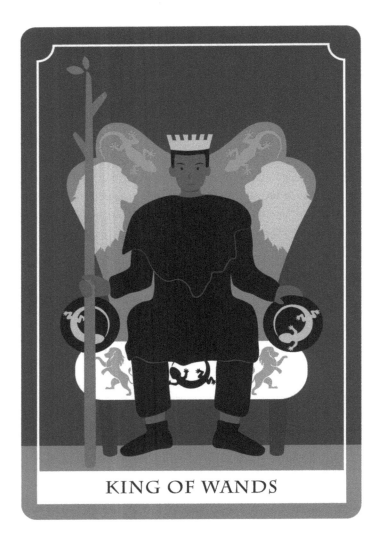

KING OF WANDS

NUMEROLOGY: Challenge

ASTROLOGY: Sagittarius

ELEMENT: Fire

COLORS: Orange, Red, Yellow, Green, Blue

SYMBOLS: Crown, Throne, Salamander, Lion, Robe, Cloak

Upright Meaning

Taking action to bring ideas to fruition with a clear, unstoppable vision is symbolized by the King of Wands. A card of masculine energy, the King is full of charisma and dedication. You are a natural at leading others and bringing visions to life. Full of confidence and acting with honor, you are able to build successful enterprises by taking an opportunity and running with it full force. Others are inspired by your manifestations.

REVERSED KEY WORDS: Anger, Recklessness, Resentment, Impulsive, Uncharitable

Reversed Meaning

Leading others is not a strong attribute when the King of Wands is reversed. You lack the confidence and skill to guide and direct. Your expectations are too high or unrealistic. You may be uncharitable toward others and acting out in anger. You may be full of resentment and behaving in a reckless manner. Your impulsive nature holds you back from success, as your energy is chaotic and without direction.

Love and Relationships

Those seeking love should stay focused and keep going with the King of Wands. An energetic, charismatic partner is approaching, and fun times are ahead for both of you. Relationships are happy, full of passion and deep love connections.

Career and Wealth

You are well respected in your career, and the King of Wands indicates success at work. You are a mentor and leader in the workplace, and this card finds your career excelling now. The accomplishments are long-term for you. Your finances are stable and balanced, with money management being a good habit of yours.

Success and Happiness

Your experience and enthusiasm will help you realize your vision. Success and happiness are possible with the King of Wands. This card shows you that your control, confidence, and leadership skills pave the way to abundance. Be sure to rest along the way.

Wild Card

Usually when the King of Wands appears in readings, you have already accomplished goals and achieved success. There are times, though, when this card asks you to acknowledge a new project or opportunity. The outcome depends on you and how much effort you are willing to put in.

A FINAL WORD

Congratulations on finishing *The Complete Guide to Tarot*! Now that you have learned about the art of tarot, your journey has just begun. Having read about the history of the cards and delved into the symbols, meanings, and background of each card and suit, you are well equipped to start reading tarot on your own. This book has given you a solid foundation to start from, including insightful spreads, and will continue to guide you and serve as a reference along the way.

I recommend practicing readings regularly to become more connected to the cards and deepen your understanding. The more you explore, the more you will read with confidence and ease. Keep a journal to record your sessions for reference and reflection. Read the cards for yourself and find others to practice on—even imaginary people, fictional characters, and pets! Take time to try different spreads, and when you feel ready, start creating some of your own tarot spreads. Have fun working with your tarot cards. Aim for enjoyable experiences.

Get creative with how you interact with your deck. Pull a card to inspire and motivate you, display a card to remind you of what you want to manifest, or choose one to meditate with for personal and spiritual growth. There are so many possibilities when it comes to exploring tarot—and yourself—through the cards.

Thank you for reading with me and taking the time to learn more about this sacred practice. Tarot offers empowerment and grounding. There is a very special connection that you build between yourself and the cards. The rituals you create and the time spent working with your deck will become a cherished part of your life. May you have many adventures and meaningful discoveries with your tarot cards.

LIST OF COMMON TAROT SYMBOLS

ANGELS represent messengers, divinity, and purity in tarot. They also show protection and higher consciousness.

ARMOR symbolizes protection, strength, or confidence. It can also indicate being prepared or taking action.

ARMS in the Ace cards signify opportunities being offered as the hands present a cup, sword, wand, or pentacle.

BEARDS portray experience and wisdom in tarot cards. Maturity and distinction are also attributes of beards.

BIRDS can reveal hope, inspiration, and knowing. They speak of higher wisdom, divinity, and viewing things from a higher perspective.

BLINDFOLDS indicate avoidance, being blocked, or denial. There is a lack of clarity or limited perception and resistance to seeing truths.

BUTTERFLIES signify change, transformation, and transition. They are also symbols of beauty and intuition in tarot.

CASTLES are reminders of achievements, goals, and good things to come. They show wealth, protection, strength, and prosperity.

CHALICES OR CUPS symbolize emotions and feelings. Love, relationships, intuition, and creativity are often associated with chalices or cups.

CHILDREN in tarot represent innocence. They depict playfulness, youth, newness, and nostalgia for the past.

CITY BUILDINGS OR TOWNS show a sense of community. They exemplify structure, order, laws, and diversity.

CLOAKS can represent different attributes based on their color. Typically, wisdom, anonymity, mourning, affluence, wealth, and being withdrawn are associated with cloaks.

CLOUDS portray thoughts, imagination, and mental states. They signify dreams and inspirations, as well as mystery and the unknown.

COINS OR PENTACLES in tarot relate to earthly matters, such as health, career, wealth, and home. Coins relate to manifestation and prosperity.

COLORS represent different meanings, often based on the chakras. The colors of symbols can enhance their meaning.

CROSSES have divine connotations, associations with life and death, and spiritual references. Reconciliation, salvation, comfort, and sacrifice are meanings of the cross.

CROWNS show power and mastery in tarot. They signify authority and indicate spiritual awareness.

DOGS show loyalty, trust, and protection. They depict camaraderie and friendships.

FIELDS reveal work to be done or that has been accomplished. They can indicate abundance, fertility, feeling grounded, or contentment.

FISH represent intuition and mastery of emotions. They indicate being in touch with one's surroundings and going with the flow.

FLAMES OR FIRE speak of passion, energy, and inspiration. Flames can also depict action, destruction, and change.

FLOWERS show growth, abundance, and fertility. They portray love, hope, and creativity and symbolize blossoming.

THE FOUR ELEMENTS are water, air, fire, and earth. They correspond to the four tarot suits: water to Cups, air to Swords, fire to Wands, and earth to Pentacles.

GARDENS convey abundance, lushness, and growth. They show a sacred or spiritual space and portray prosperity.

GRAPES represent blessings, abundance, and fertility. Grapes reveal a place of establishment or richness.

HILLS denote minor challenges or struggles. They can also signify goals or aspirations.

HORSES convey freedom and a lack of restraint. Horses show movement, strength, and nobility.

HOUSES portray security, safety, and protection. Abundance, family, and a place of retreat are also signified.

THE INFINITY SYMBOL shows immortality of spirit and the human condition. Energy is infinite and endless, and this symbol shows a balance of spirit and Earth.

LAND reveals connection to the earth, as well as goals and challenges ahead. Land indicates abundance or struggles depending on the terrain.

LEAVES represent growth, new beginnings, and fertility. Transformation is also portrayed by leaves.

LIONS express power and strength in tarot. Courage, royalty, and animal instincts are attributes of the lion.

THE MOON symbolizes intuition, femininity, and mystery. This symbol portrays psychic awareness and cycles or phases.

MOUNTAINS can depict challenges or triumphs. Mountains reveal endurance, views, goals, or struggles.

PATHS represent our journeys and the different directions we take—our choices and the route we follow.

PILLARS signify balance and a middle ground. They have spiritual connotations of life force, polarity, and duality.

POMEGRANATES convey fertility and abundance. They indicate union, marriage, and lavishness and represent femininity.

PYRAMIDS signify power, authority, and spiritual beliefs. They speak of building foundations, life after death, and higher consciousness.

RIVERS depict movement and flow. Rivers relate to direction, emotions, compassion, and intuition.

ROBES can symbolize purity, innocence, passion, intuition, and other elements. The different colors of the robes affect the meaning.

ROSES speak of purity, hope, and beauty. They depict promises and new beginnings. White roses are a sign of purity and cleansing. They depict a sense of order and beauty, as well as having spiritual connotations.

SALAMANDERS in tarot express passion, vitality, and energy. Associated with fire, salamanders depict vision, rebirth, and enlightenment.

THE SEA represents uncertainty or the unknown in tarot. Journeys and the subconscious are elements of the sea.

SNAKES indicate rebirth or growth, along with renewal. The snake represents wisdom and spirituality.

THE SPHINX speaks of guarding and protecting hidden information. This is a symbol of nobility, divinity, and overcoming challenges.

STAGES in tarot suggest maintaining an illusion or keeping up an appearance for the sake of others. Things may not always be what they seem.

STARS symbolize guidance and direction. They shine light to illuminate, indicating a higher spiritual power, faith, and hope.

THE SUN represents joy, energy, positivity, creativity, and growth. The sun speaks of new beginnings.

SWORDS convey mentality, thoughts, and beliefs. Intellect, power, courage, and conflict are associated with swords.

THRONES denote power and strength. Thrones are rigid, inflexible, and sturdy foundations.

TREES portray the human condition, strength, and growth. They signify development and the different stages of life.

WANDS represent energy, inspiration, and creativity. Wands depict passion, spirituality, and aspects of the personality.

WATER indicates the subconscious and emotions. Compassion, intuition, and healing are attributes of water in tarot.

WREATHS symbolize victory and triumph. They are a favorable sign of peace and protection.

GLOSSARY

ARCHETYPE: A symbolic representation of a certain aspect of behavior, the psyche, or life circumstances

CLEAR: To shift the energy of your deck to a more neutral state after use

COURT cards: The Page, Knight, Queen, and King in the four tarot suits

DRAW: To take a chosen card from a deck of tarot cards

INTENTION: The area of focus you would like to attract, manifest, or change in your life

INTERPRETATION: The explanation or meaning of the cards that are drawn

INTUITION: Your instinct or immediate inner knowing

MESSAGE: In the context of tarot, an interpretation of the meaning of the cards that have been drawn, usually containing insight, advice, and understanding about a situation

NUMEROLOGY: The study of numbers and their ancient mystical or symbolic meanings

QUERENT: One who seeks; the questioner, the person you are reading for

READING: The process of interpreting the tarot cards that are drawn with a question or focus in mind

SPREAD: A design or pattern of tarot cards structured to answer a question or focus on a topic in a specific way

SUIT: One of four categories the Minor Arcana in a tarot deck is divided into: Cups, Pentacles, Swords, and Wands

SYMBOLISM: The use of objects, colors, numbers, and other items to represent meanings or ideas

RESOURCES

Websites

Biddy Tarot

BiddyTarot.com

This website offers beginner tips, information about each card and different spreads to use and incorporate into your practice, online courses and blog posts, and a community of other tarot readers to interact with.

Building Beautiful Souls

BuildingBeautifulSouls.com/tarot-card-meanings

This website dedicated to the metaphysical and spiritual has a tarot section that explains the card symbolism in an easy, down-to-earth manner.

Labyrinthos

Labyrinthos.co

This website offers tarot classes and supplies, as well as brief descriptions of the cards and their meanings.

The Tarot Guide

TheTarotGuide.com

This website has easy-to-use, short descriptions of the cards to guide you in your readings.

Books

Tarot Journal for Beginners: Reflect, Record, and Track Your Insights by Dawn Marino
This guided journal helps tarot beginners connect with their decks and readings.

The New Tarot Handbook: Master the Meanings of the Cards by Rachel Pollack
This is a great book with brief descriptions of the cards and insightful tarot spreads to explore.

Tarot Plain and Simple by Anthony Louis
This book offers a more expansive look at the tarot cards and their meanings.

Recommended Tarot Decks for Beginners

Rider-Waite-Smith Tarot Deck

This is the most popular and widely used of the tarot decks. The well-known imagery and symbolism of Rider-Waite-Smith cards have inspired the creation of other decks and are ideal for beginners learning to read tarot.

Light Seer's Tarot Deck

This deck translates the meanings of the cards by using contemporary and intuitive characters in the images. The cards are expressive, magical, and full of tarot symbolism.

Modern Witch Tarot Deck

Diverse people and modern situations are presented in this updated Rider-Waite-Smith–style deck. The cards are youthful and vibrant while still holding traditional relevance in their meanings.

Superlunaris Tarot Deck

Inspiring and interesting characters make up this reworked deck that embraces modern themes. The people portrayed on these vivid and empowering cards are relatable and engaging.

REFERENCES

Esselmont, Brigit. "The Full Moon Tarot Spread and Ritual." *Biddy Tarot*. Accessed September 23, 2018. BiddyTarot.com/full-moon-tarot-spread-and-ritual.

Louis, Anthony. *Tarot Plain and Simple*. Woodbury, MN: Llewellyn Publications, 1996.

Pollack, Rachel. *The New Tarot Handbook: Master the Meanings of the Cards*. Woodbury, MN: Llewellyn Publications, 2012.

INDEX

A

Ace of Cups, 106–107
Ace of Pentacles, 136–137
Ace of Swords, 166–167
Ace of Wands, 196–197
Altars, 28–29
Astrology, 17, 35

C

Candles, 27
Chakras, 18
Chariot, The, 74–75
Clarifier cards, 47
Colors, 34–35
Connection, 15–16
Court cards, 9
Crystals, 18, 27
Cups
  about, 10, 34, 35, 105
  Ace of Cups, 106–107
  Two of Cups, 108–109
  Three of Cups, 110–111
  Four of Cups, 112–113
  Five of Cups, 114–115
  Six of Cups, 116–117
  Seven of Cups, 118–119
  Eight of Cups, 120–121
  Nine of Cups, 122–123
  Ten of Cups, 124–125
  Page of Cups, 126–127
  Knight of Cups, 128–129
  Queen of Cups, 130–131
  King of Cups, 132–133

D

Death, 86–87
Decision making, 15
Decks
  choosing, 23–25

clearing, 25, 26
connecting with, 26–27, 31–32
history of, 5–6
storing, 25–26
Devil, The, 90–91
Divination, 5

E

Eight of Cups, 120–121
Eight of Pentacles, 150–151
Eight of Swords, 180–181
Eight of Wands, 210–211
Elements, 34
Emotional awareness, 15
Emperor, The, 68–69
Empowerment, 13
Empress, The, 66–67

F

Five of Cups, 114–115
Five of Pentacles, 144–145
Five of Swords, 174–175
Five of Wands, 204–205
Fool, The, 60–61
Four of Cups, 112–113
Four of Pentacles, 142–143
Four of Swords, 172–173
Four of Wands, 202–203

G

Goal setting, 17

H

Hanged Man, The, 84–85
Hermit, The, 78–79
Hierophant, The, 70–71
High Priestess, The, 64–65

I

Incense, 27
Intentions, 3–4, 19–20

J

Journaling, 28, 29
Judgement, 100–101
Jumper cards, 47
Justice, 82–83

K

Kabbalah, 17–18, 33
King of Cups, 132–133
King of Pentacles, 162–163
King of Swords, 192–193
King of Wands, 222–223
Knight of Cups, 128–129
Knight of Pentacles, 158–159
Knight of Swords, 188–189
Knight of Wands, 218–219

L

Lovers, The, 72–73

M

Magician, The, 62–63
Major Arcana
  about, 3, 6, 7, 59
  Chariot, The, 74–75
  Death, 86–87
  Devil, The, 90–91
  Emperor, The, 68–69
  Empress, The, 66–67
  Fool, The, 60–61
  Hanged Man, The, 84–85
  Hermit, The, 78–79
  Hierophant, The, 70–71
  High Priestess, The, 64–65
  Judgement, 100–101

Justice, 82–83
Lovers, The, 72–73
Magician, The, 62–63
Moon, The, 96–97
Star, The, 94–95
Strength, 76–77
Sun, The, 98–99
Temperance, 88–89
Tower, The, 92–93
Wheel of Fortune, 80–81
World, The, 102–103
Mamluk, 5
Meditation, 19
Minor Arcana, 3, 6, 8. *See also*
        Cups; Pentacles;
        Swords; Wands
Moon, The, 96–97
Moon phases, 35
Music, 28
Mythological symbolism, 33

N

Nine of Cups, 122–123
Nine of Pentacles, 152–153
Nine of Swords, 182–183
Nine of Wands, 212–213
Numbers, 9, 34
Numerology, 33

P

Page of Cups, 126–127
Page of Pentacles, 156–157
Page of Swords, 186–187
Page of Wands, 216–217
Pentacles
  about, 10, 34, 35, 135
  Ace of Pentacles, 136–137
  Two of Pentacles, 138–139
  Three of Pentacles, 140–141
  Four of Pentacles, 142–143
  Five of Pentacles, 144–145
  Six of Pentacles, 146–147

Seven of Pentacles, 148–149
Eight of Pentacles, 150–151
Nine of Pentacles, 152–153
Ten of Pentacles, 154–155
Page of Pentacles, 156–157
Knight of Pentacles, 158–159
Queen of Pentacles, 160–161
King of Pentacles, 162–163

Q

Queen of Cups, 130–131
Queen of Pentacles, 160–161
Queen of Swords, 190–191
Queen of Wands, 220–221
Questions, asking, 36–37

R

Readings. *See also* Spreads
  card shuffling, 37
  closing, 41
  how to, 37
  mind clearing before, 36
  for others, 39
  practicing, 31–32, 41–42
  preparing for, 36–37
  reversals, 38
  sample, 40
  for yourself, 38–39
Relationships, 15
Reversals, 38
Rider-Waite-Smith deck, 6, 24–25
Ritual spaces, 27–29

S

Self, sense of, 15
Seven of Cups, 118–119
Seven of Pentacles, 148–149
Seven of Swords, 178–179
Seven of Wands, 208–209
Shadow cards, 47
Six of Cups, 116–117
Six of Pentacles, 146–147

Six of Swords, 176–177
Six of Wands, 206–207
Smith, Pamela Colman, 6
Spirituality, 4–5, 15
Spreads
  about, 4, 46
  creating your own, 55
  fear/reality spread, 48–49
  overcoming obstacles
        spread, 50–51
  past, present, future
        spread, 49–50
  personal growth spread, 53–54
  relationship alignment
        spread, 52–53
  setting up, 47–48
  two-card, 46–47
  unstructured, 55
Star, The, 94–95
Strength, 76–77
Suits, 8. *See also* Cups;
        Pentacles; Swords; Wands
Sun, The, 98–99
Swords
  about, 10, 34, 35, 165
  Ace of Swords, 166–167
  Two of Swords, 168–169
  Three of Swords, 170–171
  Four of Swords, 172–173
  Five of Swords, 174–175
  Six of Swords, 176–177
  Seven of Swords, 178–179
  Eight of Swords, 180–181
  Nine of Swords, 182–183
  Ten of Swords, 184–185
  Page of Swords, 186–187
  Knight of Swords, 188–189
  Queen of Swords, 190–191
  King of Swords, 192–193
Symbolism, 6, 10–11,
        32–35, 227–230

T

Tarocchi appropriati, 5

Tarot. *See also* Decks

about, 3–4

card symbolism, 6

Tarot (continued)

history of, 5–6

life impacts of, 13–17

origins of, 5

practicing, 10, 20–21, 29,
31–32, 41–42, 224

as a spiritual tool, 4–5, 17–19

stigma of, 16

tips, 9

Temperance, 88–89

Ten of Cups, 124–125

Ten of Pentacles, 154–155

Ten of Swords, 184–185

Ten of Wands, 214–215

Three of Cups, 110–111

Three of Pentacles, 140–141

Three of Swords, 170–171

Three of Wands, 200–201

Tower, The, 92–93

Two of Cups, 108–109

Two of Pentacles, 138–139

Two of Swords, 168–169

Two of Wands, 198–199

W

Waite, A. E., 6

Wands

about, 10, 34, 35, 195

Ace of Wands, 196–197

Two of Wands, 198–199

Three of Wands, 200–201

Four of Wands, 202–203

Five of Wands, 204–205

Six of Wands, 206–207

Seven of Wands, 208–209

Eight of Wands, 210–211

Nine of Wands, 212–213

Ten of Wands, 214–215

Page of Wands, 216–217

Knight of Wands, 218–219

Queen of Wands, 220–221

King of Wands, 222–223

Wheel of Fortune, 80–81

Witchcraft, 18

World, The, 102–103

Z

Zodiac, 35

ACKNOWLEDGMENTS

I would like to thank my husband, James, for his constant support, patience, and understanding and for all of the laughter and thoughtful gestures. Thank you for the flowers!

Thank you to Mo Mozuch for the great and insightful editing of this tarot book, as well as Beth Heidi Adelman and the entire team at Callisto Media who made this book possible.

Last, I am full of appreciation for the many tarot readers and deck creators out there who make their creations and content available, offering inspiration and collective sharing of the art of tarot.

ABOUT THE AUTHOR

DAWN MARINO is an intuitive tarot reader, psychic energy healer, and author of *The Tarot Journal for Beginners*. Her healing sessions include tarot, Reiki, crystal and pendulum healing, channeled art, and more. She works remotely with clients from all over the globe.

Dawn's tarot sessions delve deep into a person's life situations, including the action steps needed to move forward or achieve goals. Readings can focus on career, relationships, health, life purpose, and past life exploration.

She appreciates collecting and trying new tarot decks, reading books, creating art, and cooking new foods that she and her husband, James, enjoy. Dawn can be found surrounded by crystals when she is not shuffling the cards to give a tarot reading. You can learn more and contact her at HealBy-Dawn.com and visit her Instagram at @healbydawn.

CPSIA information can be obtained
at www.ICGtesting.com
Printed in the USA
JSHW011912181221
21336JS00001B/1